DATE DUE

ill 2-24-05
ill 8/8/06
SEP 11 2009

SOUTHGATE V
MEMORIAL LI
14680 DIX-TO
SOUTHGATE, MI 481

Talking With Poets

SOUTHGATE VETERANS
MEMORIAL LIBRARY
14680 DIX-TOLEDO ROAD
SOUTHGATE, MI 48195

Copyright © 2002 Handsel Books

This book was set in Adobe Garamond.

10 9 8 7 6 5 4 3 2 1

All rights reserved. No part of this publication may be reproduced or transmitted in any form or by any means, electronic or mechanical including photocopying, recording, or by any information storage and retrieval system without written permission from Other Press, LLC except in the case of brief quotations in reviews for inclusion in a magazine, newspaper, or broadcast. Printed in the United States on acid-free paper. For information write to Other Press, LLC, 307 Seventh Avenue, Suite 1807, New York, NY 10001.
Or visit our website: www.otherpress.com.

Library of Congress Cataloging-in-Publication Data

Talking with poets / edited by Harry Thomas.
p. cm.
Includes bibliographical references.
Contents: Robert Pinsky – Seamus Heaney – Philip Levine – Michael Hofmann – David Ferry.
ISBN 1-59051-018-6 (hardcover)
1. Poets, American–20th century–Interviews. 2. Hoffmann, Michael, 1957 Aug. 25—Interviews. 3. Poets, Irish–20th century–Interviews. 4. Levine, Philip, 1928–Interviews. 5. Heaney, Seamus –Interviews. 6. Pinsky, Robert–Interviews. 7. Ferry, David–Interviews. 8. Poetry–Authorship. I. Thomas, Harry, 1952-

PS323.5.T35 2002
811'.5409–dc21

2001059422

3 9082 08998 9894

Talking With Poets

edited by Harry Thomas

HANDSEL BOOKS
an imprint of
Other Press • New York

Grateful acknowledgement is made to *TriQuarterly*,
in which the interviews with Robert Pinsky,
Philip Levine, and David Ferry first appeared.

Contents

Foreword

Introducing a volume of *Paris Review* interviews, Alfred Kazin observed that all interviews are examples of biographical art, in which a writer speaks openly of himself, his background, aspirations, struggles, and doubts, or a form of Wisdom Literature, in which a writer is asked to say how we should live. The five interviews in this book seem to me to be hybrids of the two, half candid recordings, half, if not wisdom exactly, reflections on literature and life worth coming back and back to. That the five poets all speak with such glad willingness and often at such length in reply to the questions is a reflection of their good natures. It is also in some measure a consequence of the nature of these interviews. Four of them were conducted by students enrolled in a course on "The Art of Poetry" which I taught each spring for some years. Before doing an interview, the students would spend weeks reading, talking about, and writing essays on the poet's books. The poet would then come to school, give a reading, and meet with the students for an hour the next morning. The one exception is the interview with Michael Hofmann. I wasn't teaching the term he was free to come, so Professor Gill Holland, two remarkable students, Jack Livings and Geordie Schimmel, and I took him into a room, turned on the tape recorder, and posed our questions.

I am very grateful to the poets for agreeing to allow me to gather the interviews into a book. To the forty students whose names and voices appear in these pages I express now in writing my affection and admiration.

Harry Thomas
Watertown, Massachusetts

Robert Pinsky was born on October 20, 1940, in Long Branch, New Jersey, a resort town by then a bit in decline. He attended Rutgers University, writing a senior thesis on T. S. Eliot, and then Stanford, where he studied with the poet and critic Yvor Winters, wrote a Ph.D. dissertation on Walter Savage Landor, and held a Stegner Fellowship in Creative Writing. He has taught at Chicago, Berkeley, and Wellesley, and is currently a professor in the graduate writing program at Boston University. In 1995 he was elected to the American Academy of Arts and Letters, and from 1997 to 2000 he was the United States Poet Laureate.

Robert Pinsky

Jim Knowles: There's an essay by Seamus Heaney called "The Impact of Translation" in which he starts out with a translation by you. He talks about the problem a poet writing in English might have when he realizes that the kind of poem he is struggling to write has been written already in some other part of the world.
Pinsky: The poem is "Incantation," by Czeslaw Milosz, with whom I worked on various translations. Not long after Czeslaw and I had done the translation, Seamus was over to the house and I read it to him. He was struck by the same quality in it that I was. The poem is very explicit and quite, one might say, moralistic or idealistic. Could a poet in English, I thought, particularly an American poet, write such a poem? It's quite short; I'll read it to you.

Incantation

Human reason is beautiful and invincible.
No bars, no barbed wire, no pulping of books,

No sentence of banishment can prevail against it.
It establishes the universal ideas in language,
And guides our hand so we write Truth and Justice
With capital letters, lie and oppression with small.
It puts what should be above things as they are,
Is an enemy of despair and a friend of hope.
It does not know Jew from Greek or slave from master,
Giving us the estate of the world to manage.
It saves austere and transparent phrases
From the filthy discord of tortured words.
It says that everything is new under the sun,
Opens the congealed fist of the past.
Beautiful and very young are Philo-Sophia
And poetry, her ally in the service of the good.
As late as yesterday Nature celebrated their birth,
The news was brought to the mountains by a unicorn
and an echo.
Their friendship will be glorious, their time has no limit.
Their enemies have delivered themselves to destruction.

Seamus has quite complex things to say about this poem. First, he admires it rather eloquently, and then he says something like, on the other hand, this is a poem that one can imagine being written by a prelate or somebody at the seminary on the hill, some literate and bromidic Catholic: someone of intelligence and good will who isn't really hip to poetry.

Instead, "Incantation" is, somehow, a truly wonderful poem. In a way, you can say that the most difficult thing to do in a poem is to present ideas, abstract ideas of this kind, this explicitly, and attain strong emotion. And perhaps the implication is that parts of the world that have experienced totalitarian regimes are fertile ground for this kind of direct approach, while our own good fortune in not having experienced war on our terrain for over a hundred years, nor having experienced a totalitarian regime or a police state, makes us less capable of such writing.

I don't think Seamus says that, in fact, although he takes up the idea. Milosz's own opinion of that idea is interesting—he says this is like envying the hunchback his hump. He considers it a very silly sentimentality on the part of Western writers, romanticizing or idealizing the situation of the artist in extremely oppressive political circumstances. Certainly, if there is a kind of writing we admire and would like to emulate in relation to our own woes and desires, that is up to us. A lot of American poets were disappointed, as I was, that the first poet to read at a presidential inauguration since Robert Frost, Maya Angelou, read something that lacked exactly the kind of cogency or depth or impact or precision that distinguishes the abstractions and noble sentiments of "Incantation" from the clichés of journalism or from what Seamus's imaginary seminarian might write. Ms. Angelou's poem was on the side of goodness, but lacked the passion of art; considered as a work of art it had the vagueness and figurative muddle of plausible journalism at some times and the awkwardness of mere public speaking at others. But that doesn't mean that it can't be done—who knows, by

Ms. Angelou next time out, or by the poet laureate Mona Van Duyn, or whoever. Like everything else in art, it can't be done only until someone does it.

And the Heaney essay is quite subtle on the question, as I remember, and not easily paraphrased—he says something like, such writing depends immensely upon context. He says I read it aloud to him—he describes the house, he describes the moment, he's a Catholic writer of one generation thinking about Milosz, a Catholic writer of another generation; Seamus is from a country torn by violence and Milosz is from another country torn by violence, in short there's a whole context that made him especially receptive to the poem: and I think he's raising a question about context, rather than proposing to envy the hunchback his hump. It's a good essay, a wonderful essay, and I would not attempt to summarize it. I see you're nodding, so you'd agree with me that he doesn't exactly say we can or we can't write in this way.

Jim Knowles: Right. I don't think the essay says that it's impossible to write a poem like this, but Heaney does seem to say that there's a trap we fall into when we try to write a poem that sounds like a translation.

Pinsky: Yes. Yes. But I think we did a good enough job of translating "Incantation" that this translation doesn't sound like a translation, which therefore makes me think about this poem in some of the ways that I think about any poem in English that I admire. That first sentence and line—"Human reason is beautiful and invincible"—I believe I thought something like: damn it, I wish I had thought of that: and "that" could hardly mean the idea or sentiment. It must mean something more like, I wish I had found that mode and written that sentence; or, I wish I had heard that imagined music of meaning, I wish I had played that, made that sound. Which again I take to mean that it was possible: it was there to be written. The reason I couldn't have written this poem has to do with all the same reasons that I didn't write "Sailing to Byzantium" or didn't write "At the Fishhouses" but not to do with the fact that I am a Western writer or American or that I write in English. I couldn't have written this in the same sense that I couldn't have written "Sailing to Byzantium."

Harry Thomas: On this same subject, though, near the end of his book, *Czeslaw Milosz and the Insufficiency of Lyric*, Donald Davie quotes your translation of Milosz's poem "The Father" from the sequence "The World," and he calls your translation a brilliant translation, he's full of praise for it, but when Milosz came to put together his *Collected Poems* he decided to use his own flatter, more trotlike version of the poem rather than yours.

Pinsky: This is a complicated issue. Strictly speaking, the *Collected Poems* version is not entirely Czeslaw's own translation: it's largely word-for-word a trot, originally prepared by the scholar Lillian Vallee, though the note in the *Collected* says "translated by the author." Some arbitrariness of this kind in crediting translations is common, and more or less inevitable when many hands share the task. Lillian (who had very ably translated Milosz's *Bells in Winter*) generously provided her literal version of "The

World," from which Bob Hass and I worked to make our translation for *The Separate Notebooks.*

I think sometimes that a translation enters so much into the spirit of the new language that by a kind of luck it forms a new aesthetic whole; and if the author who first forged the poem deep in the furnace of the original language, and who fueled it with his heart, happens to know this new language well enough to perceive that new aesthetic whole, then it may seem to him in its formal spirit to be too much itself—even though it may be extremely close, even more or less literal: he may prefer something that is not a poem in English, that is a mere rendering, even if the rendering is not particularly more accurate, even though it may be less literal. That is the interesting part: it has nothing to do with loose or free, literal or approximate, because the issue is not accuracy or maybe even not formal equivalence—but the issue of life, an alien aesthetic life. The translation that crosses over into the poetry of the new language may be so good it is bad.

Possibly something a little like this may have occurred with Czeslaw and "The World." I remember how the spirit of that project was reflected by the way we worked, in a committee: the poet Milosz, who is bilingual; Renata Gorczynski, who is not a poet but who is also bilingual, English and Polish; and then Hass and me, neither one of us bilingual, American poets dependent upon the other two and occasional helpers like Lillian Vallee as informants. I've discovered a new phrase I like: Bob and I were metrical engineers! Also, I guess, idiom experts. This committee or writing troupe met in various combinations—two or three of four. Czeslaw used to joke about crediting the translations to The Grizzly Peak collaborative, named after his street in Berkeley, or maybe crediting them to a single, pseudonymous translator, Dr. Grisleigh Peake. I remember one day Renata said Czeslaw can't make it today. His Korean translators had come to town, and he was meeting with them, she explained. Bob and I looked at one another and started to grin. Renata said, "What's so funny?" And I said, we were just envying his Korean translators, thinking how lucky they are. She said, what do you mean? He doesn't know Korean, was the answer. So he's not there looking over your shoulder, having a view and all the authority there is.

The translations from "The World" we did in that period were much praised. People sometimes requested Czeslaw to read from them at public occasions, and reviewers singled them out when *The Separate Notebooks* appeared. This was all complicated by the fact that the originals are written in a form that doesn't exist in English. In Poland, for decades children learned to read by the use of rhymed primers. Not exactly an old-fashioned American primer, not exactly Stevenson's *A Child's Garden of Verses*, not exactly the didactic poems of Isaac Watts. Bob Hass describes the problem very well in *Ironwood's* Milosz issue. And the poems of "The World," though the sequence is subtitled "A Naive Poem," are a sophisticated response to World War II: "The World" is about Europe destroying itself. But in this "naive poem," what you see on the surface at the outset is the children, sister and brother, walking peacefully to school together. In separate poems, the children draw pictures; the mother carries a candle in a dark stairwell; the family have dinner. In another the father shows them the world, saying here's the global map, that's Europe, this is Italy, beyond the forest is Germany. He shows them the world, with a certain tone that by implication and context—making Seamus's point again—becomes in its overtones sinister and heartbreaking.

And these poems involve very simple, hard rhymes. In working with our translation committee, trying to get some of that formal note, thinking about the predominance in Polish of feminine rhymes, I made a thing that had a certain kind of rhyme in it, slanted or blunted feminine rhymes, and a certain sound, and to some degree it works, a compromise that does some little thing in English. But it does become another creature, another monster. So I can identify with Czeslaw saying, well, this thing that has slouched and slanted its way into our committee is living and breathing in some kind of half-assed way; the sense is pretty literal, but there is also this smell of an alien, English-speaking animal, and I don't want to listen to it inhaling and exhaling and grunting around in its cage, I want something more like a telephone or a conduit.

Thomas: To the original's explicit abstract language?

Pinsky: Yeah. The other thing made him nervous.

Thomas: But he seems to suggest that the tone you got through the peculiar feminine rhymes and so forth prevented you from rendering the abstract statements of the poems explicitly enough.

Pinsky: Yes, but I think it was more "technical" than that. The rhymes in Polish are plain, like the cat sat on the mat. Virtually all endings in Polish are "feminine": they end on an unstressed syllable, so it's more like the kitty felt pity. They're like that, very hard and exact, and they're very simple. The rain fell on the garden and froze and the ice began to harden. They're just very, very plain, and the ones I cooked up for the version of "The World" printed in *The Separate Notebooks* are more like—well, Czeslaw called them "modern rhymes." Here is the opening poem of the sequence in *The Separate Notebooks* version:

The Path

Down where the green valley opens wider,
Along the path with grass blurring its border,
Through an oak grove just broken into flower,
Children come walking home from school together.

In a pencil case with a lid that slides open,
Bits of bread roll around with stumps of crayon,
And the penny hidden away by all the children
For spring and the first cuckoo in the garden.

The girl's beret and her brother's school-cap
Bob, as they walk, above the fringe of bushes.
A jay screams, hopping in a treetop;
Over the trees, clouds drift in long ridges.

Now, past the curve, you can see the red roof:
Father leans on his hoe in the front garden,
Then bends down to touch a half-opened leaf;
From his tilled patch, he can see the whole region.

"Roof/garden, leaf/region"—that is our version, with the consonantal rhymes, mostly feminine. Here is the same poem in the *Collected Poems*:

The Road

There where you see a green valley
And a road half-covered with grass,
Through an oak wood beginning to bloom
Children are returning home from school.

In a pencil case that opens sideways
Crayons rattle among crumbs of a roll
And a copper penny saved by every child
To greet the first spring cuckoo.

Sister's beret and brother's cap
Bob in the bushy underbrush,
A screeching jay hops in the branches
And long clouds float over the trees.

A red roof is already visible at the bend.
In front of the house father, leaning on a hoe,
Bows down, touches the unfolded leaves,
And from his flower bed inspects the whole region.

I think that the rhymed version is fairly close, and that it's just as abstract—the literal meaning is not much different. It is not a matter of abstractions. But the *Collected* doesn't attempt the rhymes; you can just be informed that they were in the original. I think that it is the rhythms and rhymes that help create an aesthetic creature—a kind of art-organism—and it is the breathing of such a creature that perhaps must make any author nervous simply by being other. I think it would make me nervous.

Susan Wildey: Something that came up in class is that we were wondering in what way, if any, Judaism has affected your writing.

Pinsky: I'm certain that it must have, in many ways. For instance, I talked last night about my interest in things that are made, made up: I am deeply interested in the subject of creation—high and low, great and small. And religions are notable makings, religion itself is. For one kind of religious person creation itself is an episode in the career of God. For me God is an important episode in the history of creation. Possibly having been raised as an Orthodox Jew, which is to say with considerable separation from the majority culture, has contributed to my interest in making. Not sharing such creations as Christmas or Easter or the—our, your—Saviour, and at the same time having other creations like the kosher laws or the prohibition against saying or writing the word for "God": that is a richly interesting conflict. It may have increased the impact upon me of the fact that we creatures—we mammals, we colony-insects, whatever we are—have invented not only language, but Christianity and Judaism and the United States of America and the violin and the blues and so forth.

The experience of a gorgeous, fading European reality—the rich, lower-class Eastern European Judaism and its culture, which were still present and very European in my childhood—must have had an impact on me that I can't fully understand. I grew up in a nominally orthodox family. My parents were quite secular people. They were good dancers, my father was a celebrated local athlete, they didn't go to synagogue except on the high holy days. We did have two sets of dishes—that is, we did "keep kosher." And as the oldest children, the oldest son in the family, I was expected to go to synagogue every Saturday. The *musaf*, the orthodox service, lasts three, maybe three-and-a-half hours. Imagine for a moment being eleven years old: you don't like school; it's Saturday morning; you spend nearly four hours every Saturday morning in the company mainly of old men, chanting prayers in a language you don't understand, in a prolonged, accreted liturgy that is not dramatic.

What happens is an accumulation of prayers and rituals, a liturgy that feels medieval. It does not have the drama of Mass: you don't eat God. It just happens. It comes time for "*Adon' olam,*" so everybody stands up and sings "*Adon' olam,*" and then you sit down again. Time for the *Shema*, you open the curtains, look at the Torah, sing the *Shema*, close it, and sit down again. And then you sing some other prayers. Three, three-and-a-half hours. And for the old men, it's a picnic, they love it. It's a social club for them. And afterwards everybody goes down to the basement and drinks schnapps and eats *kichele*. You aren't supposed to drive on the Sabbath, so it may be one o'clock, one-thirty, before you get home. Meanwhile, outside is the great era of American baseball and the great formative era of rock and roll; across the street is a Catholic church, where they come and go, sometimes girls in First Communion dresses, they are doing something over there, something relatively brief and one may suspect dramatic, and relatively included by the majority culture.

And you just...well, I believe that for many people with Christian upbringings there's this thing I have read about in Joyce and others called a "crisis of faith" or "crisis of belief." That is not what happens in relation to Judaism, in my experience. You don't have a crisis of belief. Faith in any such sense was not something I could apprehend as a great concept in the religion. The religion is a kind of surrounding reality, no more "losable" in its own terms than the color of your eyes, or the force of gravity. It's like having faith in the universe, for the Jew to have "faith in" Judaism: it's just there. And there's only the vaguest idea of an afterlife. There's not a state of sin or a state of grace; everybody's kind of culpable vaguely and chosen vaguely. There's a merit system. You get *mitzvahs*, that is you get credited with good points, while waiting for the Messiah. Or you are credited with sins, bad points.

So you don't have a crisis of faith. You look over at the Church across the street, and you say to yourself, *hmmm*, Catholic girls and communion dresses and Jerry Lee Lewis and Jackie Robinson: it's the whole world out there, the splendid *traif* [non-kosher] cookie jar of the world. So you just turn to the world as soon as you get a chance. Or so you do if you are a child like me then. And I made a vow, I promised that little child: *once you don't have to do this, you aren't going to do it again.* They are making you do this, but when you are autonomous and you don't have to do this again, I promise you that you won't have to do it. And I am still keeping that promise. So Judaism was in large measure a powerful boredom for me, but it was a *very* powerful boredom: a serious and for me stifling force. And the force of that boredom, no mere ennui but a desperate, animal sense of being caged and trapped, left me, I think, with a feeling about the majority culture that makes me both feel more inside it than I might have been otherwise—because I chose it, I might not have, but I chose the majority culture and I like it—yet by the same process also more outside it, in my feelings, than I might be otherwise. There are special ways in which a secularized Jew feels both additionally in the new culture, compared to others, and outside it. Terms like "assimilation," or numbering generations from the first act of immigration, do not begin to deal with these intricacies.

So that's a quick sketch of my guess of what cultural ways I might have been affected by Judaism, to which I feel loyal in ways that have more to do with, say, the stories of Isaac Babel than the celebration of Passover. On the more purely religious aspects of the subject, I'd prefer to be silent right now. But to think of it theologically, exclusively theologically, would be wrong. That would neglect something else, a kind of tear-laden and enriching cultural struggle.

Ed Berman: In the conclusion of a review of *The Want Bone* in the *New Republic*, the poem "At Pleasure Bay" is mentioned, and the reviewer says that in that poem you cash in your debts to Eastern philosophy that had been accumulating throughout *The Want Bone*. I was just wondering what your familiarity with Eastern philosophy was and how it might have influenced your poems.

Pinsky: Oh, Eastern philosophy: I'm even less of a scholar of it than Judaism or Christianity. I lived in Berkeley, California, for nine years. I've done some superficial reading. Zimmerman's books about Hinduism and art are fascinating to me. I am attracted by the Hindu conception of time in the many parables where, say, Shiva will come, and then while he's talking there's a parade of ants and each ant is carrying a world, and each world has a thousand Shivas in it, and each of those Shivas is gesturing at a column of ants. They have many little parables or images like that, trying to enforce the immensity of the great cyclicalness—how everything comes back and comes back literally more times than you can imagine. And you give yourself games like that figure of the ants, as you try to imagine as best you can.

And I guess that at some point the idea I was talking to you about last night, about the way that culture is itself a kind of possession by the dead, coming back—at some point that idea illuminated for me the idea of metempsychosis, the transmigration of souls. And the way that the genetic inheritance is comparable to the cultural inheritance, each of them a constant shifting and combining of so many variables, as many variables as ants and Shivas, got connected in my mind with the migration of souls.

It is a trickle or thread that runs through this book. I suppose you could say I mock Buddha in "The Hearts." In an early draft of "The Hearts," I can remember one line that I took out was, "Easy for Buddha to say." There's that tone in the poem still, of "Easy for Buddha to say" this or that. And as I understand it, there is a considerable Buddhist tradition of mocking Buddha. It's one of the things I like about Buddhism. A Zen saying I have heard is: "Buddha is a very good stick to pick up shit with." That's one Buddha saying, and there is something awfully admirable about it; I don't know, I suppose I do think Judaism or Christianity might be better off if they had that spirit. The Torah is a good stick to pick up shit with! It would transform the religion if you could say that, if the religion were capacious enough and calm enough to embrace that.

Oma Blaise: In your essay, "Responsibilities of the Poet," you talk about the poet needing to transform a subject. Can you say more about that?

Pinsky: Bad art does what you expect. To me, it's not truly a poem if it merely says what most intelligent, well-meaning people would say. In the other direction, total surprise is babble, it's meaningless; I don't mean to say that one is on a quest simply for novelty. But your responsibility is, even it it's only to versify something you perceive as truth, to put that truth or homily into a rhyme in such a way that you are transforming it. Your job is to do something that the reader didn't already have. And this does not mean simply the lazy reader. One kind of popular fiction just spins out explicitly and doggedly the most vague, generalized fantasies the reader already has—the least individuated fantasies. The reader, on his or her own, has vague, perhaps commercially provoked fantasies of having quite a lot of money and many sexual adventures; but the nature of these dreams or of the reader as a person makes him or her a little lazy imaginatively. So someone else puts in a lot of industry, and makes up specific names of characters, and puts them in rooms and buildings and airplanes, and flies them around, and has them have illegitimate children and meet them again twenty years later, and goes through all of the laborious spinning out of the plot.

This is an art, in the old broad sense, but it is not what I mean by the art of poetry. As I understand it, soap operas take the kind of fantasy people have in common and do the work—quite skillfully—of making such fantasy material explicit, without depriving it of a vague, dreamy generality that is part of the appeal. And the reason *Anna Karenina* has a loftier reputation, dealing with very similar material to the material of soap opera, is that the material is transformed by a powerful individual imagination. It is changed by not just anybody's imagination, but by that of a great, particular transformer. The result is that the material, the adultery and money and so forth, smells and feels like something that's both recognized and strange. Somewhere in that recognition and strangeness lies your job as an artist.

For instance, a lot of people have the notion that totalitarianism contains the seeds of its own destruction, and that art is somehow linked to truth, and therefore is the opposite of totalitarianism. According to such a belief, Fascist poetry at some level would become a contradiction in terms, as in Montale's essay on that subject. And one such person with notions of that—what is the word, let's say the humanistic kind—Czeslaw Milosz, wrote in the poem we were talking about earlier: "Beautiful and very young are Philo-Sophia/And poetry, her ally in the service of the good....The news was brought to the mountains by a unicorn and an echo." That changes it; the unicorn and the echo, for example, transform the idea with a peculiar blend of irony and astonishment. And it's your job, if you are an artist, to find that moment of transformation. In contrast, sometimes people really like clichés, they really like being told what they already think.

Wyman Rembert: Can you tell us a little bit about *Mindwheel?* Something we have says it's an electronic novel or complex interactive computer game. Does it have anything to do with poetry?

Pinsky: It is a text adventure game, and I did put a lot of poetry into it, mostly borrowed. There are many poems in the game, and it was a great pleasure to see the playtesters at the company I wrote it for say, about some two- or three-hundred-year-old piece of writing, "that's neat." For example, there's a wonderful Walter Ralegh poem that you could call a riddle; it's in the form of a prophecy.

It says, "Before the sixth day of the next new year...Four kings shall be assembled in this isle" and there shall be "the sound of trump" and "Dead bones shall then be tumbled up and down." What's being described, but never named, are the play cards and dice. The charm of the poem is that it sounds like a mystical, rather frightening prophecy, and it's the cards and dice. At the end the poem says,

> this tumult shall not cease
> Until an herald shall proclaim a peace,
> An Herald strange, the like was never born
> Whose very beard is flesh, and mouth is horn.

Until a Herald calls: "...the like was never born/Whose very beard is flesh, and mouth is horn."

Well, *Mindwheel* is a narrative game where text appears on the screen; and in response to each bit of narrative, which ends with a prompt, you decide whether to go north or to look around a room, say. You type in an imperative or complete the sentence "I want to...." and the machine responds by giving you more text on the screen. Early on in *Mindwheel*, a winged person is trapped behind bars, and you—the reader-protagonist—can free this person by solving a riddle. The riddle is, "an herald....the like was never born/Whose very beard is flesh, and mouth is horn." Has anybody guessed it yet? There is a hint in the expression of insult popular when I was in grade school: "You weren't born, you were hatched." The answer is, a rooster. They play cards all night until the rooster calls: a morning herald which isn't born, but comes out of an egg; it has a beard of flesh and a mouth of horn.

This exemplifies a basic form of transformation, because the little riddle takes the extremely ordinary perception—that the cock crows in the morning and the night is over—and gives it a mystical aura: its "very beard is flesh, and mouth is horn." Ralegh's poem is a commentary on mysticism, and indeed on poetry, perhaps more than it is on the cards and dice. It is a delighted, somewhat sardonic commentary on rhetoric.

Ursula Reel: In your essay on T. S. Eliot you write: "True poetry is never really misunderstood or discarded, because its basis is in pleasure. Explanations and theories are misunderstood; pleasures are either had, or not." Can you elaborate a little bit on that and talk about the effect you want when you write a poem?

Pinsky: It's very much involved with the sounds of the words. I hope that such an answer does not seem disappointing to you, or simple-minded. I have a conviction that if you write whatever it is well enough—Wallace Stevens is a good author to demonstrate this with—the reader will put up with quite a lot of incomprehension. Look at the rooster. I think, I hope, that you all recognize that there is something appealing about the sounds of those lines. "Whose very beard is flesh, and mouth is horn" is a good line, one whose appeal may come not only before you think *it's a chicken*, but before you even think *it's a riddle*. You can sense that it's something, you get a little frisson of something interesting from it, though you don't "understand" it in the sense that you don't have "an answer" to it. You understand what kind of thing it is. Possibly before you "understand" that it's a riddle, you "understand" that it has a mystical quality, or that it sounds impressive. You come to understand *how* it's meant to make you think.

It sounds good, and it sounds good as a syntax, as well as an arrangement of consonant and vowels, and it sounds good as an unformulated recognition of other kinds of fact: the fact that "flesh" and "horn" are good words here, and the fact that horn means the substance of fingernails as well as the bony process of, say, a ram's horn, and that the ram's horn makes a pleasing connection with "herald," because it's the same word—to blow into a horn, a goat's or a ram's horn. That's how we have the word "horn," which we now apply to a sax or a trumpet, instruments made not of horn but brass. And a jazz musician will call his piano or drum set his "horn"! And so forth, through innumerable chimes and associations. A horny thing is a callous, a hardening of flesh. There is a sexual component to the flesh and horn and born and morning, and certainly to the buried image of the rooster.

All of that is operating, operating and alive in you long before you think "rooster"—or else if it isn't operating, then no amount of cleverness or profundity will make it good, will make it poetry. So that "I don't get it" is a more damaging thing than "I don't understand it," because I think often you get it long before you understand it. We are familiar with this phenomenon in music. A record comes out, and part of the pleasure of it may be that the first five or six times you hear it you don't know what the words are; then you gradually find out what the words are. But you know whether you like it or not before you understand it. The words seem to be going very well with the tune, with what the chord changes and the harmony and the instrumentation and the singer's voice sound like, and you half-perceive whether you like these words, already. It is the same with a poem by Stéphane Mallarmé.

And I don't think these things are forgotten. I think that once something really gets under somebody's skin—is recognized as really good, in the way of art—it tends to remain, always a source of what I have to call the art-emotion: whatever that feeling is that art gives to us. And this happens in the culture in general, too. Eliot is rather out of style now, particularly with academics. But he's too good, the pleasure is too solid, for his work to truly fade. Kids are still reading "Prufrock" in high school, memorizing parts of it without meaning to. It's there forever, for everybody.

Will Anderson: When you were talking about transformation earlier, I believe you used the word mystic or mystical, and it reminded me of, in "The Refinery," the idea of refined from "oil of stone," and it seemed like the imagery is sort of chemical there, but there is a sense of a wondrous transformative power. Is that the same idea?

Pinsky: Yes, it is the same idea. As I said last night, I always seek a way to experience these ideas as part of what's very ordinary. And "oil of stone" is a literal translation of "petroleum." You know, if something is petrified, it is turned into stone. And Peter is the rock you found your church on. So petroleum simply means stone-oil, oil of stone. The idea in that poem, that the transformations of petroleum—into gasoline, benzine, naphthalene, and motor oil and heating oil and all the other things it makes—WD-40 and margarine and whatever else—is comparable to the transformations of language. I mean the way language itself changes, the way it changes other things, the way it illuminates our life, and in some ways it is very toxic, quite poisonous and dangerous.

Anderson: It's a pretty volatile mix.

Pinsky: Yes, that is the sort of thinking the poem invites. It was a metaphor or comparison I liked so well that, maybe uncharacteristically, I based the whole poem upon it. The proposition is that language is like petroleum: it is dead life; it was once alive in a different way; in some other sense it remains stubbornly alive; it comes to us from the past, and we do gorgeous things with it—we wear these clothes, these fine woven stuffs and subtle colors, we have light, we have music—and there is also something terrifying about it. You are tapping an energy that can feel supremely ordinary, yet can also associate itself with mysterious awe. Explosion, gusher, leak—energy, as in a word like *fuck* or *Jesus* or *vendetta.*

Anderson: I believe you said last night that you like the mix of the high and the low. Towards the end of that same poem, "The Refinery," it seems like there's that idea, the apposition of "Lovecries and memorized Chaucer."...

Pinsky: Yes—and "lines from movies/And songs hoarded in mortmain." Varying texture in language is a pleasure partly as a reflection of the variety in oneself. My terminology of "high" and "low" oversimplifies this variety, or whatever I was trying for with "smeared keep" or "a gash of neon: Bar," or pairing "pinewoods" and "divinity"—to me, contrast, maybe even more than the richness of some single word, is a gorgeous, living part of language, like contrast in music or cuisine. The degrees and kinds of crunchy and smooth, high and low, the degrees of pungency or volume or hotness. In the refinery, they have that whole chemistry, as I understand it, that tunes a kind of hierarchy of degrees of refining. They call it "cracking" petroleum, breaking it into its components. And that is sort of like language too, maybe especially English, and maybe especially in America.

Ann Brooke Lewis: It seems that in "Window" you use the word "window" as an artifact or, as you talked about last night, as a matrix of its own, with its own history, its own part in the culture. How do you feel about the language that you grew up with personally? Do you feel that, as your Irish mother says, your house has a "windhole"? How much history or culture actually is in your language?

Pinsky: Ideally, I would like to have it all in there. I would like to speak and write a language that does not deny either my lower-middle-class childhood or all the books I've read. I am what is called an educated person as these things go. That does not negate the way I spoke when I was a child, or the way the people around me spoke in what I suppose was a small-town slum—so my mother would call it when she lamented our living there, and was certainly a working-class, racially mixed kind of a neighborhood. Just as the history of the language is in the language, the history of any person's language is in that person's speech and writing, and should be honored. One doesn't want to be limited to a pose or mode as either a pure street kid or a pure professor, because one is not pure, and the pose or mode is a confinement. As an ideal, I would like to have it all together.

And sometimes you discover the plainness in the learnedness. It is delightful to discover that the origin of a word like "window" may be something as homely or simple as "windhole." Is that a "learned etymology"? In a way, but what could be more down-home, what could be plainer? It's [pointing] the windhole, the hole where the wind comes in. Is that a piece of arcane learning, or a bit of fundamental, funky information about these brutal Anglo-Saxons in their hut with its windhole?

Something comparable is found in the lovely language of the trades, for which I have considerable affection. A carpenter won't even call it a "window." Those separate panes are the "lights" to any builder or carpenter, and the whole is also a light. And these things, the vertical members in here, are "mullions." That piece of wood, the flat piece against the bottom below the sill, is the skirt, and the movable unit with the separate lights in it is the sash. This one has an upper sash and a lower sash. And there's a parting bead between the two sashes. And a head jamb and the side jambs. And they'll use these words very unself-consciously, in the interest of clarity and precision. Hand me some more of the parting beam and the four-penny nails. Because you need to be precise. Go to the lumber store and bring me back some 3 5/8" head jamb. Or I forget what this other thing is called, face molding or something. There's some other kind of jamb that goes this way. The word j–a–m–b: is that a high word or a low word?

One more pleasing example. I went to the hardware store and bought some fertilizer. The guy says, you could buy one of these little whirling things to spread it with, but really you could just strew it broadcast. And I realized what someone from a farming background might have always known, that "broadcast" was not invented by television or radio. The word was there: it's what you do with, say, seeds. If you have a sack slung around your shoulder, and you do this [swings his arm forward], you're broadcasting. The word existed before Marconi and before TV, and for me it had been an unrecognized, dead metaphor. It's just a homey word—not archaic, for farmers, I would guess, nor for the guy in my hardware store.

Wildey: Did you write *The Want Bone* from the picture by Michael Mazur that is reproduced on the book's jacket or did you actually see a shark's jaw?

Pinsky: The image is tied to a weave of friendships that pleases me. I saw one that my friend, the poet Tom Sleigh, had given Frank Bidart. It was on Frank's mantle, and I saw it shortly before I was going on vacation to the beach—a vacation where I saw something of Mike and Gail Mazur, in fact. And I wrote the poem at the beach, remembering the bone on Frank's mantle. When Tom saw the poem, he generously gave me a jawbone too!

Later, when I needed a jacket for the book, I couldn't find an image: the ones The Ecco Press liked, I didn't like, and the ones I liked, Ecco didn't. And Mike, working from the poem and from Tom's present to me, made the picture—a monotype, a form of which he is one of the contemporary masters. I happened to be in the studio when he pulled this monotype from his press—it's a wonderful, sensuous thing to see a monotype pulled: it is a one-of-a-kind print, the plate gooey with color pressed against paper by powerful rollers, a big surface, and a motor drives the roller across the sandwich of wet plate and paper, *shhhh.* There's a certain amount of chance in the medium. If you're an expert, you can make textures that look like water or hair or smoke or these bubbles here. But you don't know exactly what it's going to look like. Maybe that is a model for what it is like to make any work of art?

Books by Robert Pinsky

Poetry

Sadness and Happiness, Princeton University Press, 1975.
An Explanation of America, Princeton University Press, 1979.
History of My Heart, Ecco, 1984.
The Want Bone, Ecco, 1990.
The Figured Wheel: New and Collected Poems, 1966-1996, Farrar, Straus and Giroux, 1996.
Jersey Rain, Farrar, Straus and Giroux, 2000.

Prose

Landor's Poetry, University of Chicago Press, 1968.
The Situation of Poetry, Princeton University Press, 1976.
Poetry and the World, Ecco, 1988.
The Sounds of Poetry: A Brief Guide, Farrar, Straus and Giroux, 1998.

Translations

The Separate Notebooks, Czeslaw Milosz, translated with Robert Hass, Ecco, 1984.
The Inferno of Dante, Farrar, Straus and Giroux, 1994.

Anthologies

Handbook of Heartbreak: 101 Poems of Lost Love and Sorrow, Bob Weisbach Books, 1998.
Americans' Favorite Poems: The Favorite Poem Project Anthology, Norton, 2000.

Seamus Heaney was born on April 13, 1939, at Mossbawn, County Derry, Northern Ireland, the eldest of nine children. His father was a farmer and cattle dealer. The poet was educated at St. Columb's College in Londonderry and Queen's University, Belfast, receiving a first-class honors degree in English language and literature from Queen's in 1961. The next year he earned a teacher's certificate at St. Joseph's College of Education in Belfast. After fours years as a schoolteacher, followed by positions at Queen's and Berkeley, he became in 1984 Boylston Professor of Rhetoric and Oratory at Harvard. He now holds the Ralph Waldo Emerson Chair at Harvard. In 1989 he was elected Professor of Poetry at Oxford, the lectures he gave there later appearing as *The Redress of Poetry* (1995). In 1995 he was awarded the Nobel Prize in Literature.

Seamus Heaney

Heaney: I really appreciate you all allowing me a morning off yesterday down in Greensboro. I got some things done that I couldn't have got done this morning.
Stephen Faller: Sleep?
Heaney: No, letters. Some letters.
Nathan Ligo: To whom do you write?
Heaney: I write letters to friends occasionally, but I do correspondence all the time. I'm at the stage of life where lots of people I know are unfortunately getting ill and some people dying. A lot of what I would call letters—as opposed to correspondence—arises out of those situations. Tomas Tranströmer, the Swedish poet, who is another person who has had his distress—he had a stroke so can hardly speak, but before he had the stroke, he said about letters, "Some letters, unless you answer them immediately, *they keep putting on weight.*" So I had some weighty correspondence to deal with yesterday.
Chris Hass: Your poems have such life on the page, and then hearing you read them last night I was impressed by

how much life, a different life, they have in the air. So I was wondering which medium, the page or the air, you think is the ideal place for them.

Heaney: Well, that's an either/or question and I find it hard to come down easy on one side or the other. As a reader, certainly, in the beginning I think I heard poetry off and through the page. I did hear it. Yet probably I was indeed what you call a page writer. I was inclined to load every rift with ore, and to forget the other rule, namely that a poem needs breathing space inside it too. As the years went on, I'd say I learned to do that second thing, to give the poem breathing space, make its medium the air. I listen out on the line. I hear it as a spoken thing more, which is going against, of course, the trend of critical theory. I'm going in completely the opposite direction. As critical practice and critical theory tend towards thinking of everything as text, I've become more and more voice/ear oriented. These poems I read last night from "Squarings," for example, I know for certain that they are more scored for speaking aloud, more open, in a more story-telling voice, than things written, say, twenty, thirty years ago. In the two little poems about Hardy, the line is not a condenser or forcer, it's more a pacer, a punctuator. Whereas I think when I was writing *The Death of a Naturalist* and *North*, the lines were denser and more force-fed with words. So yes, the weave has opened. I'm just thinking off the top of my head here, but probably the turn came after *North* into *Field Work*, where I rather deliberately went for plain-speaking lines and used the line-break more as a pacer, a timer. If you compare the poems in the first part of *North* with something like "Casualty" in *Field Work*, I think you get longer breath and more sustained syntax in the *Field Work* poem.

Hass: Are the great catalogues that show up in poems like "Pitchfork" just description after description or something more?

Heaney: It's probably an attempt to get back to relishing the words themselves. I don't know why those pile-ups occur, except, as they say, I gave myself permission to do them. I suppose if you have a meter you can do that kind of thing with more justification. That stanza, "Riveted steel, turned timber, burnish, grain" and so on, if you didn't have a meter, it might not move as well. The meter gives it drive. Isn't that the something more, the drive?

Christopher Kip: In the introductory essay of *The Government of the Tongue*, you write of the tension between art and life, between, you say, "Song and Suffering." How do you see yourself in that light, in terms perhaps, particularly, of the last section of "Station Island"?

Heaney: Both the "Station Island" exchange and the introduction to the book of essays are an attempt to represent dramatically an anxiety which is faintly neurotic perhaps, but at least it's understandable. For a good bit of my writing life I was anxious to represent the data justly and fairly. As Robert Lowell says, "Why not say what happened." That's what's going on in "Station Island" and at the end of North, the second half of North, and also in poems like "Casualty" and the poem for Sean Armstrong. But for all that poetry has to do with such painful realities, I think it has to do with pleasure also. It is song that you're involved with. If it's successful, song is perfectly in order no matter how much suffering there is, because it sings the world into a new harmony.

I quoted this thing last night from Nadezhda Mandelstam. She talks about the poet as a source of world harmony—a vehicle of world harmony, and a source of truth. These are large terms that one hesitates to apply to oneself, but her way of speaking about the function of the poet is, in general, very beautiful. She means that the poet doesn't have to talk *for* others or talk *about* them because in speaking with this hope of representing things disinterestedly, the poet is a vehicle of harmony. My representation of the song-suffering thing in the introduction to *The Government of the Tongue* was slightly pedagogical and maybe slightly reductive. I just wanted to point up the need for poets and poetry to seek what Yeats called "a vision of reality." I think a lot of writing that passes under the name of poetry is actually self-indulgent, and too self-satisfying, and kind of profiles itself in a flattering way. [Heaney stiffens, turns, and sets his face in profile.] You can hear the pathetic sigh of the self *for* itself, which is the voice of the decade or of the times. Much that is being written doesn't place enough scrutiny upon itself; it's not aware of the demands which are there in the art. On the other hand, having said that, poems have absolutely no ethical duty to stand between the goalposts of history and save all the balls that are flung at them. They can stand

and be umpire and watch them go past, put up a flag, or they can turn their back. But the poem has to know at least that there is a game going on. The poem has to understand its place and its placing, even if it is a poem of total harmony, total beauty, and apparently total innocence. Czeslaw Milosz's poem "The World," for example, is such a poem. It has been translated by Robert Pinsky and Robert Hass, but it was written during the '40s in Warsaw, during the Nazi occupation, so in spite of its naivety—Milosz calls it "a naive poem"—the poet has a sense of total world-offense going on. The poem is about trust, it's about a father showing a child a map: this is Rome, says the father, this is Prague, this is Petersburg, these are wonderful cities, this is Europe, someday you'll see St. Peter's...over the hills, there is the church, and so on. And all this is being written just as the desecration of everything these names are supposed to stand for—order, beauty, civilization—is going on. So the different sections of the poem sing sweetness, they sing innocence, they sing song; they are sing-song poems. And the sing-song is the poet's deliberate answer to the other destructive thing. Eliot said, in his haughty way, *one has to be very intelligent.* With some form of intelligence the writer is probably safe enough. But, on the whole, song, you know, that's the business. Suffering is the saint's business. I don't think artistic power is any equivalent of sanctity. They're two different orders. Certainly, sanctity in the Christian discipline involves a certain evacuation of self which is not conducive to artistic action.

Carey Morton: In an interview you say that you are an Irish poet instead of a British poet. I was wondering what you consider essentially to be Irish writing, or what aspect of your writing makes you distinctly an Irish poet and not a British poet?

Heaney: Well, the issue probably wouldn't arise at all were there not the political situation in the North. All of those remarks about Irish versus British are actually intended as irritants rather than definitions. The adjectives have nothing essential to do with the noun. They have to do with the aggravation of the political and cultural situation. They're a form of game-playing. There's no such thing as a British poet. I mean, if my books are in a library in the United States, shelved with Yeats and Beckett under British Literature, well, it's a nomenclature. Everybody understands it's an old imperial nomenclature. Fine. But in order to shift the words and the world into alignment, in order to change the game, you have to change the language a bit. And I'm gratified to see that *Irish and British Poetry* now is more common usage, in the titles of anthologies and so on. There's a new acknowledgement of difference. I just want to issue a reminder that a Hiberno-centric reading of history, culture, and politics is possible. Basically it's all part of the intimate quarrel we conduct among ourselves in Northern Ireland. In other words, it's rather like in the United States: if you take resurgent minorities, including the native American Indian, they will insist on a different reading of history. And that insistence needn't necessarily—this is the point—it needn't necessarily be based on feelings of victimization. It will necessarily be resentful in the first couple of phases, in the reminding phase. But when readjustment comes, then resentment can disappear from the minority because the readjustment has taken place. Obviously, for the minority in Northern Ireland there's been fifty years of resentment, but it's almost over, because the adjustments and readjustments are taking place. Even so, I'm still living out my own adolescent/early-manhood resentments of a situation where the BBC was the one and only public service broadcasting station in Northern Ireland. That was always an officially British thing—accents, attitudes, all the significant dates. Even the language that was spoken on the radio was the Oxford standard rather than the Ulster local. Then you'd turn on another station which broadcast from Dublin—Radio Eireann, Ireland Radio—and the accent was different. Also, the reporting was different: "The British government today said something" instead of "Today the Government." So that from the beginning I was conscious that there were two readings, two hearings, two understandings vying, but within the official culture of Northern Ireland there was no admission whatsoever that there was an Irish dimension to life in the area. Now that has changed. Also, the fact of the matter is that there was an enormous reeducation of understanding achieved in Ireland over the past hundred years and an enormous gain in intellectual and artistic confidence secured by people like Yeats, Lady Gregory, John Millington Synge, and, most devastatingly, James Joyce. Joyce challenged and subverted, as they say, the hegemony of the British novel. He changed the game. He brought Irish Roman Catholics out of inferiority anxiety into triumphalism almost. He turned their subcultural status to high cultural advantage. He said, "Okay, we may not have had the Reformation, but weren't we lucky, we escaped all the consequences. We have direct access to Dante and direct access to Europe. We are actually Greek, in a way. The Dubliner is a Daedalus. We really have bypassed the provincialism of that other island over there. And even their language, my goodness, what a hodgepodge of Indo-European messes it is!" You take *Finnegans Wake.* I mean, it's a great anti-imperial book. Joyce, if you look through the work, is merciless and accurate and hostile to English domination. His works are read in the context of international modernism—perfectly correctly—as works of experiment, as works of, once again, disinterested artistic play. But the wound of inferiority, and the wound of the Irish situation, is a *driving force.*

So, talk of Irish writing should not, after all, be conducted only in the small Ulster-bound terms I began with. The Ulster situation contains one truth, a little personal, political, tactical, current thing. But there's a bigger truth: this great secession, redress, and redefinition occurred. It's a waste of the majesty of that achievement to let it slip.

Marc Overcash: Speaking of Joyce's influence, is that why in the last part of "Station Island" it's a Joycean voice that comes out and speaks about the English language?

Heaney: Joyce is there for a couple of reasons. He's there to voice intellectual skepticism about the pilgrim's project.

"Going on a bloody pilgrimage at this stage of your life and this stage of history! What are you after? Have I labored in vain? Haven't I shown you?" The speaker has to be castigated. And in a sense he is also a voice speaking on behalf of the reader who's saying, "Now what the hell is all this about?" Secondly, for better or worse I had to have the people that the pilgrim met be people from the Roman Catholic persuasion, because they would have to be people connected by faith to the pilgrimage on the island. So that's another reason for Joyce's presence. And then too—to go back to the previous question—there is his position on song, his total certitude that getting the language into action is the best thing a poet can do. Stop fussing, he says. Have all the anxieties, but, for God's sake, transmute them. He's saying, "You just get on with your writing. That's your job. You're not to worry about it. Just do it." Poetry is do-it-yourself-language, or language doing itself through you. This Joycean position is a corrective to all the self-accusation and dolorousness and Hamletishness that the pilgrim has been indulging in. Joyce says, "It's okay, be a Hotspur of the word, lad." Joyce has this great relish. From the first word of *Dubliners* to the last word of *Finnegans Wake* the joy in Joyce coexists with the vindictiveness or the hurt or the sorrow or the sacrifice. "There was no hope for him this time"—the first sentence in *Dubliners*. And in the first paragraph the talk about the word *paralysis* being like the word *gnomon*, and so on...Yeats, you know, is a completely different kind of writer. It's an odd thing, but you never think of Yeats having an interest in words, words as occasions of relish. He's more like an eighteenth-century orator than a post-symbolist poet. He has no philological joy the way Joyce has or the way—even without reading Russian—I know Mandelstam has. He doesn't seem to have any erotic/phonetic relationship with words. He has a diction rather than anything else—*cold, passionate, dawn, horseman.* There's that set of highly charged words which are his diction. But then, by God, he has meter.

Ashley Payne: In your interview with John Haffenden you said that you saw Irish Catholicism as having a definite feminine presence. You made the comment that you saw the *Hail Mary* as more of a poem than the *Our Father.* How has that sense of the feminine presence affected your poetry?

Heaney: I used to think that my poems came out of something passive, brooding, womb-like. But the longer I live I realize that's not the whole truth. I must admit it was a kind of myth, that there was a kind of willfulness in it. These terms, of course, "feminine presence" and "masculine drive" and so on, are now regarded as sexist and suspect and agin' the law somehow. I was basing my distinctions on the biological facts of siring and mothering, you know? One is a forced entry, as it were, and the other is a suffered consequence. So you can think of poems as consequences of something, as a matter of waiting, or you can think of them as willful entering. I used to think that I wasn't a willful writer, that willfulness was somehow agin' the laws of imagination which I took from Wordsworth and Keats and the Romantics: "The spontaneous overflow of powerful feelings"..."If poetry comes not as naturally as leaves to the trees, it had better not come at all." The sense of the river Derwent licking the young Wordsworth's ear into shape: "Was it for this/That one, the fairest of all rivers, loved/To blend his murmurs with my nurse's song,/And, from his alder shades and rocky falls,/And from his fords and shallows, sent a voice/That flowed along my dreams? For this, didst thou,/O Derwent!" and so on. Without thinking of it at the time, I was totally sympathetic to that idea of poetry as something that came naturally, a process out of a condition. And I was very attracted to lines in Shakespeare's *Timon of Athens*—I took them almost as a program for poetry: "Our poesy is as a gum which oozes/From whence 'tis nourished." And "the fire i' the flint," he says, "shows not till it be struck." So in the essays in *Preoccupations* I took the fire in the flint, the Yeatsian, dominant, metrical, affirmative, commanding strength as being opposite to this kind of passive waiting. I thought of my own poems as growths, multiplying, spawn-like.

And yet, that's too simple, because all artistic work is to a greater or less extent a doing; it's an entry into an action. Well, my terms for it and my understanding of it tend to shift every ten to fifteen years—that old *dialogue with oneself*—but at present I'm very fond of Sir Philip Sidney's notion in "The Apology for Poetry" that the thing we admire in poets and poetry is what he calls *forcibleness,* his translation of the Greek word *energeia,* energy. I would say now that what distinguishes poetry is a more-than-enoughness, that it's always more, that poetry goes beyond what's merely necessary. It's an extraness. And that can manifest itself in the sheer extra force of a formal performance. Joseph Brodsky would probably think of poetry in those terms, as an inventiveness—I don't want to use the word skill, it's too demeaning—it's more a total at-homeness in the medium, a total excellence which doesn't settle for excellence, but has to out-excellence excellence. Like Byron, or like Auden or Brodsky. So that's one form of overdoing it. But even somebody like Wordsworth, whom I tend to think of as the great grey poet, has a more-than-enoughness. You think of "Tintern Abbey" and you suddenly realize, this poem is extraordinary! It keeps coming, it's full of fresh starts, and you can feel Wordsworth exulting and going with it. It wasn't written before it was written, so to speak. We tend to think of it as being there like a mountain, a serenity, a monument. But it's a poem of excitement! It was written, my God, when he was twenty-eight or twenty-nine...twenty-eight! There's the scene and then there's the exultation of memory and then there's the extraness of suddenly understanding himself at this moment, and then after that there's Dorothy, and there there's the sense that *this can go on, my God!* He's beginning to see that nature is a system of amplifying reality, and he is a part of it. There is discovery. When you hear Keats saying poetry surprises by a fine excess, sometimes you think, as I did for a long time, of Hopkins, say, or Keats himself, of the richness of language. But the excess isn't just words, isn't just linguistic texture. It's an excess of discovery or even, it can be, of formal delight. It's *forcibleness.* It's energy coming through. And you get that in a haiku as much as you get it in an epic...the surprise. With those masculine/feminine terms I think I was, perhaps, a bit prescriptive, you know...I had written an essay on Hopkins because Hopkins was deeply, deeply important to me. And I was saying in it that he was very masculine in his deliberate, forcing way with words. But, after all, he was helplessly suffering his own linguistic processes. Those words came out. It was as if the English language was hatching in him. The language had been waiting to be born again since Langland, and suddenly it came to him again. Sprung rhythm was a new birth of Anglo-Saxon poetry and the old genius of English came through again. So, there was a kind of birth-giving process there.

One of the difficulties of doing criticism by metaphor is that you get into, I get into, questions like this which I have to answer by more metaphors.

Anne Stringfield: I've been reading your translation of *Dante's Inferno.* Could you say a few words on your ideas of translation?

Heaney: Well, as I've got older I have become more concerned with the impossible ideal of fidelity, of obedience of some sort to the original. I am less debonair about taking liberties. I read last night that piece from Ovid's *Metamorphoses.* First of all, I know Latin, so I feel safe. I did my Latin homework, as it were. I looked up the glossaries, I made my own prose cribs, I tried not to pad the lines, I tried to make what I wrote true to the sense. I also didn't import images in the way I did fifteen years ago, when I did the Ugolino passage. That's the first Dante translation I did and I brought in new images, melodramatic images. Well, one that is melodramatic said, "like a famine victim at a loaf of bread." That's not in the original at all. I think that translations have more glamour as poems in the new language when there's more disobedience going on. All the evidence is there for that. You know, defeat your lexical conscience and overdo it. That will give you, if you are Sir Thomas Wyatt, the sonnet which begins, "Whoso list to hunt, I know where is an hind,/But as for me, alas, I may no more" and so on, which is a translation of Petrarch, but if you look at the original Petrarch, it's a different story. There are topazes and jewels and all of that in Petrarch. But the Wyatt poem has much much more psychological realism in it. There's much more personal presence. There's much more of what Lorca would call *duende*, that *whoosh* of personal need and lament. It's in the music of the poem, it's in the pitch of the writing. If he had been translating Petrarch *correctly*, so to speak, it would have been an enamelled allegory. I see two impulses, slightly different. One is to love the original so much *for* and *as itself* that you want to carry it across identically. Such translation is a *hommage* to the original and a prayer to the second language that it will be up to doing this *hommage*. And the second impulse is like Wyatt's, to go for a new workable poem.

There's this Renaissance poet in Polish, Jan Kochanowski, whose daughter died in childhood, and he wrote a sequence of twenty-two poems. Stanislaw Baranczak, who teaches at Harvard with me, said, you know, you should really have a look at these. They're formal couplet poems, poems of direct personal emotion, unexpected in the Renaissance, etc. etc. Anyhow, we are going to have a shot at translating them. Stanislaw, of course, knows these poems with a love, intimacy, and awe that I don't have. So no doubt he feels that the job is impossible. But even so we're going to work together. Even though he thinks that this language, this poetry, cannot go into English because of what it is in itself. Our endeavor will be to create an equivalent beauty in English. So to make the translation honor the original, I think that's a high motive, and it's often the motive, for example, of people translating *The Divine Comedy*. On the other hand, translating *The Divine Comedy* in bits as I did arises from another motive altogether. You don't know the original very well, perhaps, but you still have a vague sense of its *integritas* and radiance as a thing in itself, and you have a sixth sense that there's something there that you need as a poet, for your own creative purpose. I think that's the way Wyatt came along and sensed something in Petrarch that he needed. It's the way that Lowell came along and snatched bits out of Villon and Baudelaire and Dante and so on in the book called *Imitations*. It's a very modern, modernist way of translating. It's what Pound did with *Cathay* and *Sextus Propertius* during the time of the First World War. Here was this imperial Latin poet with an anti-imperial position, a love-elegist in a time of war. So Pound says, "Yeah, that's the poetry we need now—let's have it, let's have it. And it has to be translated this way because we're translating it for our own moment now, interpreting it, really, paying no attention—well, paying little attention—to the conventions and the otherness of the original." I worked like that on the Ugolino passage when I did it. And I also did the same with *Sweeney Astray* because I wanted an excuse to write about rain, wet, woods, and trees. In some sense, those primal, creaturely sensations are very difficult to write about nowadays without seeming to be too naive. But if you can put poems about the weather into the mouth of Suibhne Gealt, a mad figure in a medieval tale, you can appease something in yourself and still do some service for the original Irish.

The story of Orpheus which I translated, "The Death of Orpheus," I chose that because it's hard not to read it in the context of our own contemporary gender wars. In translating one word in the Latin, I did, I suppose, interpret it. My solution was both obedient and opportune. When the women see Orpheus playing his lyre, this self-entranced guy, they shout out, "Orpheus, nostri contemptor!" You can hear—even in the English if you don't know the Latin—*contempt.* Nostri contemptor: the contemptor, the person who offers us contempt. So I translated that as "Orpheus, the misogynist," which gives it a contemporary tilt, but I think it's a legitimate tilt, because in a way that's what they meant, that's what they felt. Because in the previous part of the story, we are told that Orpheus turned away from the love of women and went for...well, his bride was a young boy. So, "The Death of Orpheus"...I suppose my translation relates to the critical wars and the political wars between feminist critics and male poets: Dead-White-European-Male versus the rest, so to speak. And poor Orpheus is super-dead, super-white, super-European.

Faller: You said in the beginning of the answer to this question that you didn't take as many liberties now as you once did. I was wondering about other sorts of changes. Would you say that your poems from the beginning are growing in some way rather than changing? And if you would prefer growing—in your subject matter or style—how do you project where they're growing to?

Heaney: That's a very good question. If I had a clear answer to it, I would feel like Yeats felt after he wrote *A Vision*: totally empowered and ready to go again in my sixties. There's a little image in that Hardy poem about a ripple originating in the beginning and going out and out and out and out...My sense is that there's a certain amount of given subject matter—well, it's not exactly subject matter—it's more a locus of energy or a ground of possibility in the poet and in his or her language, and for the poet to desert that ground may be fatal. To hug it too closely would probably be fatal too. You have to move out but keep in touch, you know? Another image that I had for this in *Station Island* is of being an earthworm of the earth—leaving your mould behind you, putting the stuff through you and leaving the mould. And I suppose whatever projections I would have for my work are somehow related to those images. I would like to think that there would be a kind of life-line to the first memory-ground, but that the significance, the signification, could open a bit. Formally speaking, I would like to write more sectioned poems, not necessarily long poems. I've written two or three which proceed by juxtaposition and suggestiveness and accumulate not quite logically. They're a follow-through from those "Squarings," from those twelve-liners that keep jumping around from place to place. I would also, I have to say, like to get back to phonetic pleasure, philological pleasures, word-relish.

Courtney Robertson: Last year I was studying at University College, Cork. I took a poetry course, and your name came up a number of times. We were talking about the idea of women as nature and men as culture in looking at "Digging." How do you respond to that critical argument?

Heaney: Well, it's a critical language, it has a new approach. Patricia Coughlan has written an article, a polemical article, about that. And it's necessary that those inherited tropes be interrogated. Nevertheless, poetry isn't just its thematic content. Poetry is in the musical intonation. What is missing in a lot of that criticism is any sense of the modulation, the intonation, the way the spirit moves in a cadence. It deliberately eschews the poetryness of poetry in order to get at its thematic and its submerged political implication. That's perfectly in order as a form of intellectual exercise and political protest, but it is not what the thing in itself is. Within this new critical dispensation, Rilke's "Sonnets to Orpheus," you know, could be taken to task for silencing the little girl who is the occasion of them—the child who died. You could see a fierce political point being made against Rilke for this. At the same time, the Sonnets refuse the terms of that argument. This is the old argument between, if you like, truth and beauty, put in another way. Or between the Puritans and the playwrights. That criticism is very Puritan: extirpate the mistaken because we are in a new world of understanding and character. This is a pattern that keeps repeating. But I think it's a fair comment, within its own terms.

In fact, the Orpheus poem is a response to that development. Once again, it's rather scampish. That poem is published along with a translation of another poem by Brian Merriman, a late eighteenth-century Irish poem. I did a little book in Ireland before Christmas, called *The Midnight Verdict*, including extracts from this late eighteenth-century Irish poem called "The Midnight Court" by Brian Merriman. It is a thousand-line poem, a survivor of a medieval genre, a dream-vision poem. The poet is summoned to a court by a woman bailiff, and the court is run by women, and the President of the court is a woman, Aoibheall. She's sort of a faerie guardian of Munster.

And the women are there to protest against the men of Ireland because the men are paying insufficient sexual attention to them. It's not a poem about romantic love, it's a poem about frustrated sexual appetite, and it has all of these old, traditional motifs. Any scholar of medieval literature will detect them: *the chanson de la mal mariee*, the cry of the young woman who is married to the old man, and the lament of the old man against the young woman, and all of that stuff. It's full of vigor and interest and then, at the end, the women get a verdict in their favor and the poet is to be tied to a gravestone and whipped and all the young men are to be whipped, and so on. But then, of course, the poet wakes up and he escapes. Then it struck me that if you listened to this poem within the acoustic of "The Death of Orpheus," you'd have a very interesting amplification going on. And if you set it in the context of this kind of criticism, and relate it to the resurgence of women and the vehemence of the Women's Movement in Ireland, then you have dialogue, you have answer back, and you have provocation. Why not? It is a dialogue. Patricia Coughlan did an article on the passive woman figure in the representation of Ireland. But, in fact, English armies did come in and do all that depradation and the Irish poets of the eighteenth century were remembering Elizabethan scorched earth and Cromwellian massacre and took that image of violation and rape pretty seriously because, I mean, these were not just literary tropes.

Ellie Brown: I'm curious about how you feel your time spent in America has affected your writing. Has it changed your thinking about Ireland?

Heaney: I don't know the answer to that. I think it has changed my writing a bit. I'm not sure that it has much affected my attitude to Ireland, because Ireland, Northern Ireland in particular, is a form of entrapment that nobody can help you with. And it has to be known from the inside. Outsiders can solve it like that [snaps his fingers]! Solutions straight away—bang, bang, bang. Why don't you dee dee dee? Why didn't you da da da? Because...[Heaney does a Neanderthal slump and stare]. I think my being here might indeed have affected my writing...made me ready to improvise a little bit, to open up and to skim along. I think the poems in *Seeing Things*, those twelve-liners, might have something to do with—not with the influence of American poetry—but with the space-walk aspect of my own life here. I think being here might have added more confusion than clarity to my understanding of things...Speaking, I mean, in literary terms. Within my first ear, within my first literary hearing, because my ear was formed by British, Irish, English, Scottish literature and rhythms and meters and sounds, I would be intolerant of a lot of the open-weave talkiness of American poetry. But since coming here I've realized that I respond like that because of my first closed and tense expectations. I've realized it's part of the American idiom, it's part of a different culture, it's part of a different project, a different ambition. So I've got a kind of laissez-faire now in myself towards things that I was agin' in the beginning. I'm not sure whether that is a gain or a loss. I think that as a reader you can have tolerance that you mustn't allow yourself as a writer. You can listen in and say, "yeah, yeah, yeah," but you mustn't admit that to which you say "yeah, yeah, yeah" into your writing because then you become untrue to yourself. I mean, all you have to go on as a writer is your sixth sense and your sense of the world and your ear and your instincts. There are many other things which you can include or address, but if as a poet you're not on the beam, if you aren't coming in on the radar system that belongs in your own ground, you're not actually destined to land safely. Maybe I've been overly fearful of opening up to other influences. I can *hear* a lot going on, but I don't let it into my own writing. There are only two or three references to the United States in all of my written work. It's not that I'm against it. It's just that I haven't found a way to get at it. I was delighted to get Bay Bridge and Berkeley and San Francisco into one of the little "Squarings." Well, you know, that's an interesting thing. When Derek Walcott, a mutual friend of Harry's and mine, did a book that was called *The Fortunate Traveler*, dealing with his migration to the United States, the theme was totally interesting to me, but the poems kept reminding me of Elizabeth Bishop. It's something about the landscapes. Derek wrote about England in another book called *Midsummer*, which is more credible musically, because Derek is to a certain extent an English poet. He's got the canonical pace of the pentameter deep inside him. The verity of your note is important. On the other hand, a poet like Czeslaw Milosz can encompass California and Lithuania. But that was suffered for. Milosz came to California but his being in California was by no means a matter of good luck and bonus—which is how I would regard my presence in the United States. I came in my forties to teach. I spent a year at Berkeley as a young parent and a young poet. But I was going back home at the end of the year. So my relationship with this country is one of enrichment and extraness. If you take a writer like Milosz, however, it's one of tragic destiny and fierce historical irony; he, whose sense of gravity is over-loaded with the tragic, ends up in the Bay Area, among the hippies and the flower people. He was living not in history; he was living in some kind of marijuana Limbo. And therefore he ponders and finds the ground of his understanding of the twentieth century in two places, historical Europe and emancipated America. California was the locus of some kind of new knowledge. It happened to be the place where a rebirth and an aftermath took place. So, the American thing, the American locus, and the American settings were life-changing for Milosz because he made his home here. I live in Ireland. I really haven't changed. I haven't moved, I haven't left, I just come for the visit. It's a completely different relationship with the place. And I must say that I feel the impulse to stop that, feel the impulse to go back and pull down the blinds and stay at home. [sotto voce] Too late?

Ligo: You referred a moment ago to a poetic sixth sense, and you discussed the artistic self and the potential conflict between that self and the world. Do you still feel some conflict arising in your life between the need to hear this inner self and, say, religion or just people around you who aren't paying heed to it?

Heaney: I think that's a need that's in everyone. It's to do with individuation, as Jung might have said. It's to do with coming through, as Lawrence would have said. It's to do with integrating, to do with the problem of being one person, as Milosz says. He says in his poem "*Ars Poetica*?", "Our house is open, there are no keys in the doors/and invisible guests come in and out"—but even so we'd like to be one person. But where do we begin this oneness? Where do we start building towards oneness? I think everybody in some intuitive or inchoate or deliberate way seeks answers to those questions. The fact of the matter is that for me the confidence-building and the sense of touching base in myself came from writing poems in my twenties. My first poems were very important to me in grounding some sense of identity.

I think the question of faith is separate. You can keep your faith or lose your faith. Those traditional terms mean something. I suppose I lost my faith. That is to say, I stopped going to the sacraments and living within the terms of a system of belief and a system of practice, a system of coherence, a system in which everything was ordered. That, perhaps, cannot be replaced. And all the talk and all interviews and so on, they are ways of saying we're making the best of it alone and, we hope, inventively.

I hate the thought of this being transcribed. I also feel sorry for whoever must transcribe it. [He looks around the room] Will you all take turns at it?

Harry Thomas: That's a thought.

Heaney: It's a very difficult thing to do.

Faller: Especially the incorporation of gestures.

Heaney: Yes, that's true.

Faller: And the expression of things which aren't said.

Heaney: That's correct. That's why one must rewrite it, because a spoken intonation can carry weight. Brodsky—Joseph Brodsky again, whom you've probably met with

Harry here—has this wonderful statement in his introduction to translations of the Russian poet, Alexander Kushner. He talks about tone and intonation, and he says, "Intonation, which is, as it were, a motion of the soul."

Which is lovely. We were talking about themes and music and so on. Tone—this is a phrase of Eavan Boland's that I really like—tone, she says, is a kind of index of the writer's relationship with the suffered world. Oscar Wilde's tone, for example, is very light, but there's a sense of a relationship to a suffered world that isn't frivolous. It's perfectly light, but it's clued in. "There's no such thing as a moral or an immoral book. Books are well written or badly written, that is all." That isn't as innocent as it sounds. Well, it sounds innocent, but there's the back echo of experience also. "To fall in love with oneself is the beginning of a life-long romance." [Laughter] Yes, this is Oscar, and you understand that there isn't just the joy, but that there's self-accusation lurking there too, that behind it there is, as Boland says, a *suffered world.* Which is wonderful.

Books by Seamus Heaney

Poetry

Death of a Naturalist, Faber and Faber, 1966.
Door into the Dark, Faber and Faber, 1969.
Wintering Out, Faber and Faber, 1972.
North, Faber and Faber, 1975.
Field Work, Faber and Faber, 1975.
Poems 1965-1975, Farrar, Straus and Giroux, 1980.
Station Island, Faber and Faber, 1984.
The Haw Lantern, Farrar, Straus and Giroux, 1987.
Selected Poems 1966-1987, Farrar, Straus and Giroux, 1990.
Seeing Things, Farrar, Straus and Giroux, 1991.
The Spirit Level, Farrar, Straus and Giroux, 1996.
Opened Ground: Selected Poems 1966-1996, Farrar, Straus and Giroux, 1998.
Electric Light, Farrar Straus and Giroux, 2001.

Prose

Preoccupations: Selected Prose 1968-1978, Faber and Faber, 1980.
The Government of the Tongue, Farrar, Straus and Giroux, 1988.
Crediting Poetry: The Nobel Lecture, Farrar, Straus and Giroux, 1995.
The Redress of Poetry, Farrar, Straus and Giroux, 1995.

Translations

Sweeney Astray: A Version from the Irish, Farrar, Straus and Giroux, 1983.
The Cure at Troy: A Version of Sophocles' Philoctetes, Farrar, Straus & Giroux, 1991.
The Midnight Verdict, Gallery Books, 1993.
Laments, Jan Kochanowski, with Stanislaw Baranczak, Farrar, Straus and Giroux, 1995.
Diary of One Who Vanished: a song cycle by Leos Janacek of poems by Ozef Kalda, Farrar, Straus and Giroux, 2000.
Beowulf, Farrar, Straus and Giroux, 2000.

Anthologies

The Rattle Bag: An Anthology of Poetry, selected with Ted Hughes, Faber and Faber, 1982.

The School Bag, edited with Ted Hughes, Faber and Faber, 1997.

Editions

The Essential Wordsworth, Ecco, 1988.

Philip Levine was born on January 10, 1928, in Detroit, the second son of parents who immigrated to the United States from Russia. He attended the local schools, Wayne State University, the University of Iowa, where he was a member of a legendary workshop taught by John Berryman, and Stanford, where he held a Jones Fellowship under Yvor Winters. From 1958 until his retirement in 1992 he was a celebrated teacher of literature and writing at Fresno State University. Among his many awards are the National Book Award for Poetry for *What Work Is* (1991) and the Pulitzer Prize in Poetry for *The Simple Truth* (1994).

Philip Levine

Chris Wyrick: Congratulations on the big prize! [The Pulitzer Prize in Poetry for *The Simple Truth*]
Levine: Well, thank you. Yes. It's been a long time coming. But, you see, patience does pay off. Actually, I think it's better to get it when you're old. Ah, I'm happy to win it.
George Weld: I think now especially a lot of young writers feel a tension between the feeling that they need to be activists in their work for social change and a feeling that, as Auden says, "Poetry makes nothing happen," that poetry is irrelevant or elitist, and I'm wondering whether you feel this tension yourself.
Levine: Well, frankly, I think that Auden is wrong. Poetry does make things happen. And I think that if a young person is troubled by the idea that he or she is practicing an elitist art, then he ought to do something else. I mean, if you have grave doubts about being a poet because you will thereby not achieve your social ambitions, then don't write poetry. Poetry will make it without you. And the question you have to ask yourself is, "Can I make it without poet-

ry?" And if the answer is fussy and hazy, do something else. The answer had better be loud and very clear: "I can't make it without poetry." Because there's so much in a life of poetry that can defeat you. And the apparatus for rewarding you is so abysmal, and the rewards themselves, aside from the writing of the poems, so small, that there's no point in doing it unless you're utterly confident that's your vocation, that's your calling. I was very lucky when I was your age. T. S. Eliot came to see me. He said, "American poetry just needs you, Phil." He took the bus. In Detroit. I was surprised to see him in a Jewish neighborhood, but there he was. I said, "You're Tom Eliot." He said, "Say Sir, son." Of course, I'm kidding. It was a long bus ride from London, from Faber and Faber.

When I was your age I had no doubt. I also had social goals, and I was naive enough at eighteen or nineteen to think that poetry or fiction could have a vast social influence because it had a vast influence on the way I felt and thought. I was aware of the fact that while I was reading poets like Eliot, Auden, Spender, Wilfred Owen, Lowell, Stevens, and Hart Crane, my neighbors weren't.

They wouldn't have known who the hell I was talking about, so I didn't talk about them. I'd guess much of my family was puzzled. They must have thought, "What is this infatuation and how long will it last?" I was the only member of my family ever to finish college. There's a Yiddish expression that translates, "For this you went to college?" That's exactly what my grandfather said to me when I graduated from college and told him I wanted to be a poet. He told me about this man who lived in his village back in Russia before he left in '04 to come to the United States. This guy was some sort of lunatic who went from house to house; people fed him and listened to his terrible poems. My grandfather said, "At least he didn't go to college. Why did you go, for this?" I tried to explain to him that I didn't go to college to become a poet, that while I was there my romance with poetry deepened. He just shrugged.

But poetry does make things happen. You know that already. It changes all of us who read it. But it will not change legislation.

Rachel Newcomb: I have another question that's along those same lines. In an interview in 1988 you said that perhaps American poetry had stopped believing in itself, and I was wondering if you felt that contemporary American poetry has become marginal and, if so, how can poetry attract a larger audience?

Levine: I don't know why I said that in '88. I can't recall the occasion. Perhaps I was reading a lot of boring poetry. I talk to a lot of younger poets and most of them don't seem to feel their generation has found itself yet. I had a conversation for publication recently with a wonderful younger poet, Kate Daniels—she must be thirty-eight or so—and she felt her generation hadn't yet found what it wanted to do, but she felt that my generation had to assert itself early because we were under the shadows of the giants. If you looked at the magazines in which I first published, you'd see I'm in there with Stevens, Marianne Moore, Williams. I wasn't awed by them. I knew how good they were, I knew they were writing far better than I, but I thought, given enough time, they will vanish from the earth in their bodily incarnation and then maybe my writing will get as good as theirs. Well, the first part did happen, and I'm still waiting for the second.

You asked about the audience for poetry in our country. I think it's the largest it's ever been. I know we're told otherwise. There's this "expert," Joseph Epstein, who published something like *Who Killed Poetry?* or something like that. Nobody killed poetry. Guys like Epstein like to hearken back to some dreamland America in which people got up in the morning and opened their windows to the birds singing and when they felt their souls elevated they recited American poetry to the waiting world. Bullshit! If you go back to the time when Stevens, Eliot, Williams were first publishing, exactly the same things were being said in the middlebrow press: "Look at this generation of turkeys. You can't understand a word they write. They're so obscure and so negative. Give us back our uplifting verse!" That was the middlebrow response to one of the great outpourings of poetry in the history of the English language, which took place early in this century.

What happened in American poetry was extraordinary: Frost, Stevens, Williams, Pound, Moore, Eliot, all writing at the same time, E. A. Robinson, the whole Imagist thing. And the Epsteins of that hour were griping just as they are now. My guess is that today it still has something to do with class; they can't stand the idea of all these poets coming out of Turkey Tech and Fresno State and Puma J. C. They're from the fancy places that once owned our poetry. We had the same response from the Eastern lords when the Beats hit the press.

I think poetry now is very healthy. There is no such thing as an official style. It's open house. It doesn't matter how tall or short you are, what color you are or what sex you are or what nine sexes, you can put anything in your work.

You can write about anything. No matter how badly you write you can find somebody who'll publish you. Time will sift the good stuff from the bad. As far as readership goes it's the largest it's ever been. I know, we're told no one is reading it, but that's nonsense. Go back and discover how large, say, an edition of William Carlos Williams was in 1944. His last book, *The Wedge*, was published in fewer than 500 copies. In '54 his great book, *The Desert Music*, was published by Random House; I'd be surprised if they did more than 1,200 copies. How big was the first edition of Lowell's incredible *Lord Weary's Castle*? One thousand copies? Berryman's *The Dispossessed*? I'd bet fewer than 1,000. The first edition of my new book is 7,500. And Sharon Olds and Adrienne Rich outsell me; they must do 10,000 of theirs. My editor told me the other day that Galway Kinnell's *The Book of Nightmares* had sold 60,000 copies and is still selling. I remember a year ago reading with Galway in Portland, and afterwards they had a book-signing, and for over an hour people kept lining up with old battered copies of his books. Those books had been read, God knows by how many people. There is a huge readership. We're told otherwise by the naysayers, but it's not true.

Patrick Malcor: You said that there is no specific style of poetry right now. Do you think poetry is beyond the point where it can have a movement, a certain mass style, or do you think that it needs that?

Levine: There will always be movements. We have one right now that began in California, the Language Poets. Do you know their work? [Blank looks] You don't, God bless you. Young poets begin movements to have something to belong to, something potentially exciting: "We're going to change American poetry!"

Ever since I began writing I've noticed that certain movements are there mainly to help people without talent write something they can pass off as poetry. If you can't tell a decent story, denounce poems that tell stories. If you can't create characters, denounce poems with people in them. If you can't create images, write boring generalities. If you have no sense of form, imitate the formlessness of the sea. If you have no ear, disparage music. If everything you write is ugly and senseless, remind your readers that the world is ugly and senseless. Bad poets are incredibly resourceful. But those are movements that are easily forgotten. About fifteen years ago we had something called the New Formalism, and it seems to have vanished already. Very curious movement, a sort of nostalgia for the poetry of the fifties and perhaps the decade itself, and it occurred at a time when the best formal poets of the fifties—Wilbur, Merrill, Hecht, Nemerov—were still writing incredibly well. The important movements change the way we see poetry or poetry sees us.

When I was your age a poet friend of mine, Bernie Strempek, and I founded a revolutionary poetry movement. We called it The New Mysticism; that was Bernie's idea. I believe he truly believed in the majesty and burning of the invisible whereas I was about as mystical as a sofa. Clearly we didn't change anything, not even the way we saw ourselves, but for a few weeks we had great fun talking about how we were going to change the country. Both the Language poets and the New Formalists strike me as less interesting than the New Mystics, though I am hardly objective. They're such conservative movements: neither seems in the least interested in shouldering a social or spiritual or political agenda. Both are academic and largely praised by academic critics and by the poets themselves, but perhaps they will have a healthy impact on our writing. They probably find my work and the contemporary work that resembles it garbage, which is fine. What's important is there is not a single official, accepted style. Today someone entering poetry can take any number of directions and find other poets who will validate his or her work. I hate the notion that any style, mine or anyone else's, is *the* style.

We have had very important, essential movements in this century. For me the most important one was the Imagist movement, which included such poets as Williams, Pound, Ford Madox Ford, D. H. Lawrence, and profoundly changed both English and American poetry. One in England right after the end of World War II changed the entire focus of their poetry. It was labeled "The Movement" and was something of a repudiation of the high-flown rhetoric of poets like George Barker, Dylan Thomas, and Henry Treece. Suddenly we got these hard-assed poems from poets like Thom Gunn and Philip Larkin. They seemed more interested in what went on in a department store than what went on after you died and went to heaven. They'd write about trying to pick up a girl or spinning out on your motorcycle or finding a pair of pants that made you look sexy. In their poems people sound like people and not holy texts. In "Church Going" Larkin writes about a man with no religious faith who goes into an empty church and wonders what the hell it's for. At one point in the poem he says "up at the holy end"; he can't think of the name for that part of the church, if he ever knew it. It's a marvelous poem about the need for religious feelings in people without religious feelings.

And then in the late fifties we had the Beat or Black Mountain thing, all the poets represented in Donald Allen's anthology *The New American Poetry.* If you can still find that book, have a look at it. You'll find it contains some of the best American poets of the second half of the century: Gary Snyder, Creeley, Ginsberg, Robert Duncan, Denise Levertov. All of us who write poetry owe those poets a great debt for ending the absolute domination of the official Eastern establishment; that was a great service. Maybe you folks would like to start a movement: the Davidson Suicide Squad or the North Carolina Stompers. It couldn't do any harm, and it might enliven things. They're a little dull right now.

Todd Cabell: You mention in the first essay in your book,

The Bread of Time, that anybody can become a poet, that we have democratized poetry, and then you mention creative-writing classes in colleges and schools. I wonder, being a teacher yourself, what exactly do you view as bad in that movement?

Levine: Nothing. I think it's a wonderful thing. When I started writing there was not the sense that everybody could become a poet. Chicano poetry did not exist. Asian-American poetry did not exist, such giants as Robert Hayden and Sterling Brown were not represented in the official anthologies. I'm having fun in that essay, and I'm also being serious because I do think there are too many writing programs and many are staffed by people who can't write themselves. I visit places where poetry is taught in graduate programs, and I can't believe the level of the writing. Then I see the poetry the teachers write, and I know why. And you visit a class, and everything is praised: the MO seems to be, "Let's pretend all this writing is poetry." Once you create a program you require students, so you let everyone in and you keep them in by making them happy. I also visit writing programs in which real standards are operating, the students have talent and are reading and working like mad; the teachers are dedicated, demanding, fair, and they are gifted and productive poets themselves. There are two things you must have for a valuable writing program: first and most importantly, the right students. Then the teachers. You could have mediocre teachers if you had great students because the students will teach each other and inspire each other. The problem is great students rarely gravitate to mediocre teachers.

Wyrick: I'd like to ask a question about your method of writing. In *What Work Is*, in the poem "Scouting," you say, "I'm scouting, getting the feel of the land," and in the poem "What Work Is," "Forget you. This is about waiting, shifting from one foot to another." And I want to ask you if you could tell us more about this process of scouting that you engage in your poems.

Levine: That's a difficult and interesting question. How do you research a poem, which is what scouting is? Or at least that's one of the things I'm scouting for in the poem, the poem itself. You know you're constantly obliged when you apply for grants or things like grants to describe the specific steps you're going to take to write the book you're asking for financial support to write, and of course you rarely know exactly what you'll have to do. If you've been doing it as long as I have, you have some idea, and I'd call it a kind of scouting. It's a circling and circling, quite literally—a cityscape, a landscape, a subject, an emotional obsession. I'll give you an example. I have this fascination with Spanish anarchism, so back in the seventies I went to one of the great collections of anarchist literature, The International Institute for Social Study in Amsterdam. The records of the CNT and the FAI—the National Workers Confederation and the Iberian Anarchist Foundation—were stored there. Most of the stuff is in Spanish, and at the time my Spanish was good enough to read it. The people who worked in the library there were very helpful and generous; they brought me whatever I wanted to see, old newspapers, posters, memoirs, manifestoes, anything I asked for, and I sat there for hours, day after day, reading. The poetry I finally got had nothing to do with Spanish anarchism, though I have written many poems out of that obsession; this "scouting" produced poems that had to do with being in a library. They had to do with the quality of light, the sadness that invades a library late in the afternoon when you've been there all day from 9:00 in the morning until 5:30 and suddenly you realize the light has changed and the day is ending. In Amsterdam the weather can change very suddenly, and I would glance out the window and dark clouds were blowing in from the North Sea, and the day was totally different from the one I left when I entered the library. My heart was always yearning to go out in the streets and to be in Amsterdam; it's such a beautiful and lively city. I learned a hell of a lot about Spanish anarchism and I wrote about my hours in the library, the people I met there, the yearning for the city, the shocking realization of how quickly time was passing and the light going.

And "Scouting," the poem itself, is about my days in North Carolina, your dear state, where I lived the summer of 1954 in a mountain town called Boone. I thought I'd made a drastic step that might mean I would never become the amazing poet I had seemed destined to become. I had just gotten married. I had fallen in love with a woman who had a young child, and so we married. I thought, "Look what a foolish thing love has driven me to do. I must now be a responsible human being. I'm only twenty-six years old and I've thrown my young life away." You know, men at twenty-six are total idiots. I would go for long walks most days. I didn't have to work, my new wife was working and supporting all of us. I was supposed to be writing poems, but my mother-in-law had come for the wedding, and no one can write with his mother-in-law in the house, even, as in my case, if she's a lovely woman. So I went on these long walks and began to discover the landscape of those mountains and the people. I'd knock on doors of these little cabins and say, "Could I have a drink of water?" And besides the water, which I always got, I'd get different responses. "Where are you from, son?" "What are you doing here?" They'd hear my accent and know I was not local, these gracious country people sharing their water with me, their time; we'd have wonderful conversations. It was a kind of scouting. As I got further and further into it I realized I was carrying out research, I was researching myself as well as these people and their place. My mother-in-law left, so in the mornings I'd work for hours on poetry; I found Saintsbury's *History of English Prosody* in the local library, never had been read, pages uncut, and I poured over that. I'd been trying to write poetry for ten years, and I still didn't know how to do it and knew I didn't know. But I was getting clues and I was also learning how to research poems: you keep your eyes open, your ears open, all your senses open. The world responds to you, and you respond to the world. It goes on that way, it never ends.

Keats has a late letter to Shelley. I don't think he ever

truly cared for Shelley. It might have been a class problem, Shelley coming from the rich and famous family and living his "spontaneous" life. Like Byron, Shelley wrote all the time. Keats had long bouts of silence, what we too easily call writer's block. He suggests to Shelley that his poetry might be richer if he "loaded every rift with ore," if he wrote less and did it with more intensity. He goes on to say that he has sat as long as six months without writing. I think Keats believed, as I have come to believe, that not writing is part of the process of writing. Not in the beginning—for first you have to learn what the hell it is you're doing—then you must write, as Berryman said to me, everything that occurs to you.

I've been very lucky. I've never had one of those terrible droughts. Three or four months is the longest I've ever gone without writing poetry or something I could regard as poetry. I've come to think part of the process, an essential part, is waiting, being patient, and avoiding what one might call busy work. There's the temptation to construct what you secretly know is second-rate and keep working at it because it beats not working at anything. I think you're better off not writing at all than just soothing yourself with busywork. I'm not talking about beginning writers; they have no idea where anything will go and should plow ahead with whatever comes to them. By the time you've been at it fifteen years you know when you're just imitating yourself.

"Scouting" is also about that dreadful moment here in North Carolina when I said to myself, "Philip, you have o'erstepped your usual timidity and entered upon marriage." You know I was just like any other jerk my age. No one had told me how to become a poet, and I'd figured out that if you didn't have money there were two ways to live: you can have a family or you can write poetry, but you ain't going to do both. How the hell are you going to take care of kids, help dress and feed them, get them off to school, and then write a poem? What kind of nonsense is that? I figured I should have someone coming into my study with toast and tea, I should have silence interrupted at intervals for wonderful meals. Wasn't that how Rilke lived? How many nights do you think he sat up with a sick kid? You know at one point or another in your life you have to wake up and become a person. The irony of all this is I was incredibly lucky. I was marrying a woman who had a profound regard for poetry and this kid I adopted turned out to be one of my best friends. It was probably one of the three or four intelligent decisions I've made in my whole life. Another was buying the house I work in in Fresno. Another was not going to the Korean War. I can't think of another one, but there must be a fourth.

Mary Stephens: I'm interested in how memory works in the writing process because so many of your poems are retrospective. How does this process differ from poems that are observed at the moment of conception? And how important is looking back, not only on your own experiences, but on your earlier writing?

Levine: I don't know if I can answer the second part. It seems to me that you made a distinction between writing a poem that would come out of memory and one that would come out of an experience that was before you. But you'll notice that in my poems it almost doesn't seem to matter what's before me: I go back into memory and try often to twine what I remember with what I'm observing. And I'm not sure why I do this, although it's obviously something that I do. I think that a lot of it has to do with the fact that I feel an urgency to record things because they seem so transitory. And I am now a kind of archive of people, places and things that no longer exist. I carry them around with me, and if I get them on paper I give them at least some existence. And that seems like a legitimate thing to be doing with poetry. To be granting some form of permanence—I mean, however permanent the poems are—to the things, to the way of life and the people who made up that way of life.

As far as looking back at my own writing, I try not to. I purposely don't memorize my poems. When I'm on the brink of memorizing a poem I stop using it at readings. I wait for time to erase it because I don't want to memorize it. I don't mind memorizing other people's poems, but I'm not going to sit down and write a poem that I've memorized by Hardy or Wyatt or Dylan Thomas. I'm not going to do that. Whereas a poem that's my own may haunt me if I go back to it. I don't want to go back to it. I don't want to look at it. And sometimes when I look at them I'm a little depressed by the fact that they're better than what I'm writing now. That's another thing: I believe some of the older poems have more imagination, more vitality. I know that these last two books have won all these honors, but I actually prefer some of the older books.

People ask me, for example, what's the book I'm working on now, what's it about, and when I tell them the truth they think I'm putting them on. I say, "I don't know yet. I won't know until I'm done." But that's the truth. That's happened with every book I've ever written. I didn't know what the book was about until I finished it or got close to finishing it. And then I saw, "Oh, that's what I've been obsessed with!" For example, in writing the last book, *The Simple Truth*, I saw at at certain point that there were three poems I needed. I had taken out a group of poems that either weren't good enough or didn't belong. I said to myself, "I need three poems to go right there," and in the next month I wrote them. That was very rare for me.

With the book *What Work Is*, I suddenly realized I needed a long poem at the center, so I revived a poem I'd been working on for at least a dozen years and had failed to finish, "Burned." I looked at what I had and knew the time had come to finish it. And I got it. I didn't get it right, but I think I got it as right as I would probably ever get it. Sitting over it another year wouldn't have made it any better, so I let it out into the world. And it was well treated. Have I answered your question?

Geordie Schimmel: What if not poetry? If not the dialogue with stars and trees at thirteen, what would you have chosen?

Levine: It would have been the dialogue at fourteen. That's what I was going to do. I don't have the least doubt about it. Before I was ten I was utterly fascinated with language, with the shape and flavor of words. And I got so much pleasure from using language, and I used it with snap. Besides, there weren't that many other options. I couldn't have been a dancer, I'm too awkward. I can't draw so I couldn't have been a painter. Maybe an Abstract Expressionist, except my sense of color stinks. I can't carry a tune worth a damn, so although I love music it wasn't for me. I might have become a critic. No, never a *cricket*, as Mark Twain calls them. Better to be an honest huckster and sell Buicks. I might have become a novelist. When I was in college I worked as hard at fiction as I did at poetry, but back then my temperament wasn't suited for it; I hadn't yet developed the incredible patience a novelist requires.

William Robert: I'd like to return to your works for a minute and ask you a question about them. Pretty consistently, from the earliest ones to the ones that just came out in *The Simple Truth*, you develop many philosophical threads. And one of the most fundamental seems to me to be the lack of, the impotency of, even the impossibility of, true communication between individuals. Do you see this as an ironic stance for a poet, namely one who depends on communication, to take?

Levine: No, no, I don't. Failing to communicate is part of what we live with, part of our condition. Poetry is about as good as we can get at communicating without the aid of gestures, without the aid of our bodies. Rilke wrote somewhere that without our bodies we cannot love. Also with our bodies, with our gestures, with our facial expressions, we can communicate far more fully than with merely words on the telephone or in a letter. Poetry is as close as we can get to complete communication with words alone. And I think it's good enough. I believe that when I'm reading Keats or Hardy—another of my favorite poets—I'm getting it, the essence of what they have to say and even more than the essence, lots of the particulars. Obviously I'm not getting it all. There's no such thing as perfect communication. Hardy's experience of the world is not mine, though our lives overlapped by some months. Keats's experience of the London of his era is not mine; their experience with the words they use is so different from mine. But the miracle of poetry is that it can cross so many of these barriers. Approximate communication seems so amazing itself when you consider how separate we are or how separate we have conceived of ourselves. I believe that we aren't nearly as separate as we think we are. If, for example, someone in this room were running a fever we would all heat up a bit, we'd feel it even though we might not know we felt it. Our eyes tell us we're more separate than we actually are, and our conscious experience tells us, and we've conditioned ourselves to believe we're more separate. But to get back to poetry, given who we've created out of ourselves, poetry is miraculous.

But you're right: there is an obsession in much of my work with the failures of people to communicate, but those failures are usually very specific. I'm usually concerned with a few people, perhaps only two, and how they fail to communicate. A book that moved me enormously when I was young, maybe eighteen, was *Winesburg, Ohio.* I remember a story about two very lonely people, a man and a woman, who have no one to communicate with and whose experience of love is very limited. As I recall—I haven't read the story in ages—they get together and they discover they have these mutual needs and they could be dear friends. As I recall the man oversteps the bounds of this budding friendship; while the woman is trying to speak out of her joy that she has a listener he shuts her up by kissing her. There's this awful and wonderful irony that he has chosen to communicate his love or joy in the occasion this way, and she wants to communicate it another way and you can't do both at the same time. She says something like, "But, Harold, let me tell you what it was like to be six and a solitary girl," and he goes smack, smack, as if to say, "Let me show you what it's like to be twenty-seven and a man in the company of a woman." I thought Anderson had captured something amazing: how even when we fail each other the miraculous happens, they cross that great divide that separates one person from another. I believe it's possible. I believe I've done it, totally. I try to record it in my poem "The Escape." The communication between the speaker and the woman is total, and he becomes a creature endowed with two sexes, an angel with no wings. They don't do it merely with words, but they do it. He touches the woman and discovers he's also touching himself because they've become one being.

Kristina Nevius: Through this interview you've mentioned languages. What effect have foreign languages and cultures had on your poetry?

Levine: When I go to a foreign country where I don't speak the language I usually make no effort to learn it. I'm just "The Ugly American," as Eugene Burdick called us in his novel years ago. I enjoy the ignorance. I use it. Say I go into the Campo Fiori, the great open market in Rome. I stop and listen to two people standing in line to buy eggs. The man says to the woman, "Was there ever a more perfect shape than an egg? And the luminosity! The amazing delicacy of the color, the way it takes the hues of the air. Not only does the egg contain sustenance for us, for our bodies which feed our souls, but within each egg is the potential of a creature that can fly." Amazing, they say such rare things in such common places in Rome; Italians are angels. Of course that's not what they're saying at all. The guy has turned to his cousin Elfonzina and said, "Holy shit, the bastard raised the price again!" Because I don't speak Italian I've endowed him with poetry, and I say to myself, "How fortunate you are, Philip, to be living among such profound people when in fact they're saying the same trivial things they'd be saying in Fresno or Detroit."

One invaluable thing I learned from studying Spanish was how great our own poetry is, how many things it can do that Spanish poetry hasn't done. We appear in American poetry and we speak in our daily voices. It gave me a new regard for American poetry. Discovering the great poetry written in Spanish in this century was intoxicating. There's also much more awful poetry written in Spain than in the U.S. because anyone who goes to the university in Spain publishes a book of poetry. The dentist will hand you a beautifully printed book of poems—each dentist has one—all about the perfume of flowers, the brightness of the moon, the tenderness of kisses, the sweetness of the night air of Andalusia, the kindness of wild herbs. The poetry of love, dreams, moonlight, fantasy. Absolute garbage. It's so bad they couldn't even sing it in Nashville, and they can sing anything in Nashville. The great poetry is able to use the same vocabulary and break all the silly conventions and astonish you.

Even though I had to work like a demon on my Spanish, I got a great kick out of being able to speak it and understand it. I also found it exhausting to speak it for hours on end. One day I got so tired I went into a little park near the *futbol* stadium in Barcelona, flopped on a bench and slept for hours. Once I started dreaming in Spanish I got scared I'd lose my American English, so I would go down to the port and speak to American sailors and marines off the ships.

I think, too, it's very good to read poetry in another language to discover the immense possibilities we're not taking advantage of in our poetry. I know you can discover much of that reading translations, say of Zbigniew Herbert or Tomas Tranströmer, but I think you get an even keener sense when you read someone like García Lorca or César Vallejo in the original. And you're inspired in the same way you're inspired when you read Whitman or Dickinson or Williams. I can still recall struggling with the poems of Miguel Hernández in the original and those sudden glimpses of how astonishing the poetry was, how brutal and lyrical at exactly the same moment. I'd never read anything like it; it reconfirmed my belief in the power and beauty of poetry in the face of the worst life can dish out. These are poems that grew out of the most tragic circumstances. They are full of indescribable pain, which he foresees. They are very great and very difficult poems; I had to work hours, and then I would get this glimpse of their majesty. Going to Spain, living there, was a wonderful experience for me. I owe the discovery of the poetry mainly to Hardie St. Martin, the poet and translator I met in Barcelona. He was working on his great anthology, *Roots and Wings*, and generously took me into his stable of translators.

Alex Crumbley: Did it take you long to become comfortable writing persona poems? And when you do, do you have the trouble with people assuming you're the narrator when you're not?

Levine: First thing, it didn't take long at all. Once I decided I wanted to do it, I just did it. I had written a lot of fiction, at least a dozen stories and large chunks of two novels, so I was used to the problems of getting into the heads of other characters and getting them to speak in my writing.

As far as people misreading, I don't much care. I remember a review I got, I think it was in the *Village Voice*, in which a woman wrote that one of my poems from *7 Years from Somewhere* was very curious. The poem, "I Could Believe," is in the voice of a guy who has come back from the Spanish Civil War. This woman wrote something like, "Levine is an autobiographical poet, so it's amazing to discover that he fought in the Spanish Civil War, which ended when he was eleven." She mused over this, and then wrote, "Perhaps he's trying something different." Perhaps if I'd written in the voice of someone coming back from the American Civil War she wouldn't have missed it, but you can't be sure. If you're troubled by being misunderstood then you'd better not publish.

Even our fellow poets and friends read our poetry differently. I remember going to a class at the University of Minnesota and having a conversation with them; it was much like today. At the end someone asked if I would read one poem. I said, "Sure, let me read something I'm working on and we'll see what you think of it." I read "Listen Carefully" in an early draft. After I was done a young woman asked me if I would publish the poem. I said, "Yeah, if I ever get it right." "But if your sister read it, how would she feel?" I said, "I don't have a sister." She was shocked. My host, Michael Dennis Browne, an English poet who has become a fine American poet, then told an interesting story.

He said, "You know, Sharon Olds was sitting in that same chair last year, and for some reason she got on the subject of Phil's poetry. She told us how she had asked Phil where she might get 'chocolate cookies in the shape of Michigan,' cookies Phil refers to in one of his poems. To Sharon's surprise Phil said he just made it up." Michael quoted her in a surprised voice, "He made it up!" as though that were unheard of. Sharon is a dear friend of mine, and my guess is she was having fun. It's very possible it's not something she would do in her own poems, but I'm sure she knows it's something I do all the time. To me it's always open house; it you want it and it doesn't exist, just make it up. This poem with the cookies in it is about an amazing kid, a kid so amazing he's not human and yet he is. He's what human beings would be if human beings were totally themselves. Now how would I know what human beings would be if they were totally themselves? I'll tell you how; I've been totally myself. I've experienced it. That's what you become when you're inspired, you become totally yourself. We pray to the muse and all the rest of that.

Poets tell us, Coleridge and Keats for example, that they wrote some of their most inspired works when they were invaded by a force not their own. Maybe they're right, but I have a different notion: I don't believe there is this outside force. I believe that we are so rarely totally ourselves that when we are we don't know who we are. I think it's similar to what athletes refer to as being "in the zone."

That's what poets live for, those days when we are totally ourselves. I know when I'm there. I awaken in the morning, and I know I'm there, that today it's going to happen. I've been working toward that day for ages, and when it comes I'm in no hurry. I learned from Alberto Giacometti to take my time when *the* day comes. I think it was in 1968 I read a book called *A Giacometti Portrait*, by James Lord. One chapter describes a day on which Alberto knows he's going to do great work, he just has it, so he just goes about his day very slowly. He wants to touch and perhaps bless as much of his daily life as he possibly can, the people and the places and the things that make up his daily life. He takes a long walk, he visits his usual haunts, he talks to people, and then he gets down to work. I had no idea you could do that until I was forty or forty-one; I didn't know the poem wouldn't run away from me. When you're inspired there's no rush; it's who you've become. Take your time, move around, absorb all you can, reach out as far as possible. You're not going to lose it. It's there. It's you.

Books by Philip Levine

Poetry

On the Edge, Stone Wall Press, 1963.
Not This Pig, Wesleyan University Press, 1968.
5 Detroits, Unicorn Press, 1970.
Pili's Wall, Unicorn Press, 1971.
Red Dust, Kayak Books, 1971.
They Feed They Lion, Atheneum, 1972.
1933, Atheneum, 1974.
The Names of the Lost, Atheneum, 1976.
Ashes: Poems New and Old, Atheneum, 1979.
Seven Years from Nowhere, Atheneum, 1979.
One for the Rose, Atheneum, 1981.
Selected Poems, Atheneum, 1984.
Sweet Will, Atheneum, 1985.
A Walk with Tom Jefferson, Knopf, 1988.
Blue, Aralia Press, 1989.
New Selected Poems, Knopf, 1991.
What Work Is, Knopf, 1991.
The Simple Truth, Knopf, 1994.
Unselected Poems, Greenhouse Review Press, 1997.
Mercy, Knopf, 1999.

Prose

The Bread of Time: Toward an Autobiography, Knopf, 1994.

Translations

Tarumba: The Selected Poems of Jaime Sabines, edited and translated with Ernesto Trejo, Twin Peaks Press, 1979.
Off the Map: Selected Poems of Gloria Fuentes, edited and translated with Ada Long, Wesleyan University Press, 1984.

Interviews

Don't Ask, University of Michigan Press, 1981.

Editions

The Essential Keats, Ecco, 1989.

Michael Hofmann was born in 1957 in Freiburg, Germany. His father was the professor and novelist Gert Hofmann. The poet was four when he first came to England, his father taking a teaching post for a year at Bristol. Three years later, after a stint in Edinburg, the family returned to Germany, but Michael enrolled as a boarder at Winchester, one of the most prestigious English public schools. In 1976 he entered Magdalene College, Cambridge University, where his tutors were the poet J. H. Prynne and the renowned scholar and critic Christopher Ricks. Since 1983 he has lived in London as a freelance writer, reviewer, and translator. His numerous awards include the Geoffrey Faber Memorial Prize, the IMPAC Dublin Literary Award, the Schlegel-Tieck Translation prize (twice), and the PEN/Book-of-the-Month Club Prize for his translation of Joseph Roth's *The Tale of the 1002nd Night.*

Michael Hofmann

Geordie Schimmel: I have a question about *K.S. in Lakeland*. Most of the books I've seen—*New and Selected Poems*—include poems by book, but you haven't done that. You've rearranged them. Why is that?
Hofmann: Well, it's not really a Selected. Selected from two books, two and a bit books. Still, it gave me an opportunity to rearrange things and to make it like one new book, and I wanted to do that. The father things all had to go together, and there are things I wanted to put together anyway. There's a poem called "Body Heat" and a poem called "Changes" that were in different books, but that sort of go together, and I wanted to put those in relation to each other. I was sitting in my garage room in Mexico, spreading things out, photocopies of everything, and arranged them. In '89. It was wild.
Harry Thomas: In your recent review of Donald Justice's *New and Selected Poems*, you write, "There is a sense, I suppose, in which all poems have to be 'literary', although the concept of 'literary' is capable of indefinite extension

to accommodate even what was once resolutely unliterary." Do you see yourself as writing resolutely unliterary poems?
Hofmann: I did. I did. I started off with sort of anti-literature—no line-breaks, no music, no repetition. Just matter, I think, matter. And then I was sort of seduced by the whole enterprise—seduced by music, rhetoric, pleasingness. I desperately wanted not to please when I set out. My only concession to pleasing was wit. I think of poetry as being like a swamp. The poet will go into it thinking you can preserve your dryness, or your abstemiousness, or your ickiness about it, but actually you're getting bogged down in it...blub blub blub. I said yesterday or the day before that I'm sure you end up espousing positions that are the opposite of what you went in with. I haven't yet written rhyming strophes, but I wouldn't exclude it the way things are going.
Thomas: Joseph Brodsky said to me years ago that he hoped you would do that at least once, demonstrate your technical proficiency by writing a severely formal poem.
Hofmann: At least once...
Thomas: Do you see that as a seductive possibility?
Hofmann: Now that I've been told that. I don't know if it's seductive, but...yes, to prove that I can, to please a ghost. I knew an Austrian writer who wrote some short books and he once referred to those as *Talentproben*, proofs of talent, evidence of talent, a test. I did rhyme once, when I translated *The Good Person of Sichuan*. The songs in that rhyme, or many of them do. That was tough. Not least because the model or the blueprint that I had in my head

is a different one: it's pop songs or hymns, so things would come out with rhymes that sounded trite, as in a pop song...It's difficult, but I couldn't exclude it. Gawd!

Jack Livings: Do you think that has had something to do with your father's fame, growing up with the weight of literature in general on your shoulders?

Hofmann: Yeah, I do. I think that's quite a good thought. The poems started off being very short and sort of anti-poems really, little footnotes on everyone, appearances. I think that the first thing I ever wrote, called "Calm and Reasonable Complaint," was like that. Then, of course, your ambition kicks in, and you want not only to write little darts, little squibs, but, you know, you want to get in everything, all your words, everything you know, feel, and think. There's that sort of omnivorousness of the enterprise. And it's something which is related to the quicksand-like nature of it, but it's not the same as that. The one you do to please yourself, the other to please the art. And I'm not trying to do that yet.

Gill Holland: You said "seduced by music." That reminds me of what you said about Karl Miller. You called him your Sibyl, said that he had said only two words to you: once, reportage; later, music. I suppose that's the Karl Miller who's written about doubles?

Hofmann: That's him, yes.

Holland: Well, I'm wondering about that double, that sort of tension: music on the one hand, reportage on the other.

Hofmann: They felt prophetic at the time. When he said reportage I didn't know particularly what I was doing or what I ought to be doing, and that sort of confirmed me in doing this. This is just a little after the anti-poems. And music being so much the opposite of that....It seemed like an outrageous, heretical thing for him to say really, but I went and did it. Or he saw that I was doing it actually before I did.

Holland: You say it sounded almost prophetic, these single-word commands?

Hofmann: Once I was looking for his address, and I found his note to me. He'd just written "Cumae" on top. So he was up for the part.

Holland: I've always liked Kurt Schwitters, and I think your poem, "Kurt Schwitters in Lakeland," is wonderful, especially the way it ends. Harry asked about the severely formal, but in its way this poem is severely formal—although it's not metrically formal—the final picture here on his *Merzwall*: "It too was moved,/ cased in a steel frame, and keelhauled down the hill./ The one thing still there that his hands had touched/ was a stone on the sill/ of the picture window that had been put in in place of the wall. It had an air/ of having been given a spin,/ a duck, a drakkar, a curling-stone." Magnificent!—even though I still haven't been able to find out what "drakkar" is.

Hofmann: It's like the duck and drake; drakkar is a play on duck and drake. Drakkar is supposed to be, as you probably know, a longship, a Norse dragon ship. It's something I'd known, or thought I'd known, for a very long time. It just describes the form of the stone, and it suggests a little bit about Schwitters' itinerary through Scandinavia. It was a parabola that your existence makes if you're displaced or a vagabond or something like him. And it's a poem about his life through the islandbaum, fetching up in the Lake District. How he was buffeted around, his vicissitudes. Even after he was dead!

Schimmel: It's interesting, the word vagabond. You said in your reading last night that you feel like a foreigner wherever you are. And yet you write so much about place, so much of your poetry concerns place. No place is yours and you claim all these places in your poetry. That reminds me of Kurt Schwitters, creating something, assembling something.

Hofmann: Oh, I think very much so. I mean, they're relics really, the objects in his pictures, aren't they? Bus tickets and postcards and things...And the poems are sort of my relics. I don't have a title to a place either, but I have the little stub of the ticket that got me there, and that's what these things are. There's choice in the matter and no choice. I moved around a lot as a child—one school for a couple of years, then another. And then the pattern gradually slowed down. I studied in Cambridge for seven years, and I've stayed in London for the last ten. But I think in my head I see myself as rootless or...a pendulum swinging from place to place. I don't know. In the poem I wrote that invokes Joseph Brodsky, I saw him sitting in a cafe in London, working, and nobody knew he was there....It was some time ago.

Holland: That's "An Education"—"Brodsky, sitting in the window, with paper and a cigarette,/the recording angel,/ miles away."

Hofmann: For me, that's the image of the poet—the poet

as transient and responding to whatever place it is. I find it hard, I suppose, though, to write about the fixities of my own situation. I couldn't imagine being in an upstairs room in Munich, writing out of that, being nourished by that for any time. You know, the most stereotypical poem I've ever written is "A Brief Occupation": "one night, the last thing in a bare room." That's the Michael Hofmann experience. There's nothing dogmatic about it; everyone's had this experience. But I think it is what I know, and I give a little yelp of recognition when I see it, when I see, say, Brodsky in his sublime orbit. I've translated a couple of books by Wim Wenders, and he doesn't like being stuck anywhere either. He likes being flighty, and it gets him going—traveling, driving, sitting in trains, having the landscape move past you. This is the century of movement, displacement, whatever. Isn't it? Reverse Descartes for me!

Livings: It's like looking from the outside all the time. I hear that from a lot of people who go abroad for the first time, for an extended period of time. They say that all of a sudden their home becomes so much clearer to them because they're not there any more; they see so much more clearly.

Hofmann: Most of my things were written when I was away. Either in Germany or Mexico—anywhere out of this world! I've probably never written anything at my poor desk.

Holland: Is that part of your fascination with Rilke?

Hofmann: I think he sort of took it too far. You know, you can't get fussy or prissy about where you are. And so I finally get rather exasperated with him arriving in Spain in 1912 and immediately being gar...gar...what does he say?...something like always falling asleep from quandariness. Do you know the phrase? "And after almost falling asleep from quandariness," I think it says in "The Day Lady Died." So I think Rilke feels so much of O'Hara's word "quandariness" that when he gets to Spain, he thinks, "God, ought I be here? Ought I not to be in Sweden, ought I not to be in a German spa?" And I think, Jesus Christ, just be there, relax, forget it, it doesn't matter. I mean, he's looking for this appointed place, this higher place, and I never do that. That preciosity; that mission; I'm forever ending up somewhere randomly. *Fleeting:* I think that's the difference.

Thomas: I was struck in reading "Going East" and poems like it by what seemed to me an odd way you have of referring to events and figures in German history as if they were as familiar in English, to English, as English events and figures, or as familiar as they would be if you were writing in German. There's an effect almost of irreality at times and great anxiety, especially when it's clear you're writing in Germany.

Hofmann: Yeah, I love that. Irreality, definitely. I am struck by the way things straightaway lose their authenticity when they're taken out of one language and put into another. And, you know, if you wanted to make something of it, I think you could say that because I write in English and my first four years were spent in Germany and German was originally my first language, everything I write has this shimmer of inauthenticity or anxiety. That's what Germany is for me. I remember an electrifying feeling, being in Hamburg for just one day, the "pylons walking through the erasure in the Bayrischer Wald" ["Fine Adjustments"]. You said anxiety, didn't you?

Thomas: And of course the use of German words simultaneously with the use of translated German words adds to this shimmer, as you call it.

Hofmann: Well, I suppose the German words appear in some sort of edenic way, even though they're these grim places like frontier crossing-points and so forth. I think that's how it is. I remember Mandelstam's Acmeism: nostalgia for world culture. Or all the bits of this and that in Modernism. This is like a crummy version of that.

Thomas: Have you written any poems in German?

Hofmann: I wrote two or three during a period of maximum German when I was about twenty. I think they are different. I love German, and to me German is, not just because of its being my first language, but I think it may be a more expressive language for me than English. I'm being half-serious about this. I think English is handicapped by being half-Latin, and the Latin/Greek half is gradually decaying. People don't know it. It's like words like *etiolated* or *decimated* are used to mean pretty well anything, whereas in German you have this sort of absolute clarity you follow and work in. You can even have your coinages, and every child can still tell you the meaning of the word.

Thomas: Like, say, *gastarbeiter*.

Hofmann: Yeah, yeah. Or somebody pointed out to me the other day that *Heim*, the word for home, is contained in *Geheimnis*, which is the word for secret. So you think of the strange connection between the word for secret and the word for home. Home is where you have no secrets; your home is a secret.

Holland: *Heimat* is a magical word for Germans.

Hofmann: Yes, completely...I'm gradually incorporating more German words. When I started writing it felt like cheating. I have this English code of honor that told you that if you have some particular advantage it isn't right to use it. So I didn't have any German. But I suppose I have some belief in the ultimate relevance and helpfulness of having another language even when I wasn't using it. And on my ultra days I want to propound that you can't write with just one language. Or half a language, as I'd have to contend that English is for many of the people who write in it. But even when I feel more concessive, I think it's useful, it helps. I think play is very important in all that—you can have a language that you play in. So I mean that even if English is basically everything to me, I can still play in German, play with German. Maybe that's why I like German as much as I do.

Holland: That's homo ludens....In your review of Muldoon's *Madoo: A Mystery*, you mention sympathetic ink. Well, I'll walk a hundred miles to talk to anybody who mentions sympathetic ink. What a great concept! And I thought of sympathetic ink when you were talking about going to different places and Rilke and then about *Geheimnis* and home. There's some sort of sympathetic resonance between these words perhaps. And when you've got two languages working in one poem, there's a secret.

Hofmann: I think so. There was a time when I had the

idea, I'm writing alternate words, and I thought of calling the book of poems *Macaronics*, which is that. It's Kauderwolsch and half dog-Latin. I think...does anyone know what the Beefheart song is? "My home is where my..."? It's not "wherever I hang my heart," but it's..."My hat is my only house when it rains."

Holland: *Heart* is?

Hofmann: No, it's some sort of variant, probably some variant on that. But I was thinking that, with me, language has to be portable; it's what I carry around with me. It's sort of reality. So when I come into my godforsaken rooms that I write about, where I unpack, where I hang up different words on the wall, that's to give me the feeling of...again in German we say *Geborgenheit*, security, from *bergen*, to shelter, though to my wicked ear it sound like it has something to do with *borgen*, which is to borrow.

Holland: So you actually put the words up on...

Hofmann: As it were, as it were. That's what I would have to do because that's what I carry around with me, and that's how I establish my identity, and that's how I reflect myself, you know, to make me feel more *plastisch*.

Holland: Well, now I think that's what some of those Chinese exile poets you were so hard on in your review of Seth's translations...

Hofmann: Well, that....[laughter]

Holland: Well, had some rather damaging comments about....[laughter]

Hofmann: I love Chinese poetry. Chinese poetry is one of these irreducible things, I think. Whenever I read something really good, say, Akhmatova, it seems to have a sort of percentage of what to me seems to be Chinese poetry. Or it has the sort of Chinese feeling. Man in space. A bundle of memories and feelings and senses in a vast void. I think those things are just perfect—tiny, physical notations, obliquity, and an absolutely direct emotional statement at the end. "Cho-fu-sa."

Holland: Well, I was just thinking about what you said about Vikram Seth's translations, which I thought quite interesting. The best Chinese translations, you said, have a certain inauthenticity in English—the Pound, the Rexroth, and so on, but Seth's translations were presented as *echt*, conservative, and that, I would agree, is incomparably worse. They're presented as the "real thing,"when we all know that they not *echt*.

Hofmann: This isn't really something I know a lot about, but I think it tends to be a bad sign when books of Chinese poetry come with long notes and present the Chinese *en face*. I think you're in for a hard time when you read them. Whereas *Cathay*, it's sort of flagrant; it declares the inauthenticity of the words, and it's perfect for what you get. And I suppose I would say that's always more or less what you're going to get in English. When you get the great imports, when you read, say, Marquez in English, you get a Latin Americanized flavor, *Einschlag*. It's not real Columbian or real Chinese, but it's from the extremities of English. It's got on leather chaps and a flat black hat, and wow, you think, this is great.

Holland: Well, I think some of that comes across in *After*

Ovid, which is why it's so good. It doesn't pretend to be *echt* and conservative.

Hofmann: I think what we were hoping for was something like "Sextus Propertius" or *Cathay*. But especially "Propertius," because that's the classical version. I think that the people who got on with it best were the Irish. They seemed to have a more natural affinity with myth, or they could understand it. Something like Muldoon's "The Lycians," which has this wonderful way of beginning just in midstream: "All the more reason, then, that men and women/should go in fear of Leto...." So you get both a sort of fake narrative sound and then the stories within the stories within the stories with a sort of mythic gloss, a mythic take on history, on life. That just seems to be something they can do more naturally. Whereas some of the English and Americans are knocking out things that are more like standard translations, not quite what we'd hoped, though there's some wonderful writing in there. It's a great feeling to sit back and have things come in through the mail. I remember thinking, this beats writing!

Livings: We were talking earlier about Nabokov. What do you think about authors who translate their own work into English—Nabokov, Milosz, Brodsky?

Hofmann: I suppose the only person who I've sort of seen both ends of the process with is Enzensberger. His *Selected Poems* came out lately, and he did some of the translations, and he handles himself with great freedom. A translator tends to do what he's given, but if what you're given is you, then you can fiddle around with it, and do all sorts of things. He did this thing I mentioned the other day where he translates "lawnmower," or whatever it is, as "toothbrush." And there's even a sort of rationale then, because both words expressed a certain hope or confidence in the medium term future. These things were both useful for keeping up appearances. I think he just got bored with "lawnmower," and said, "Now it's a toothbrush." And I think you can do that, and you have to follow the genius of your other language. I think Brodsky does that. I haven't read that much of Milosz. I don't know really, but I think of the liveliness of Brodsky, everything comes alive. He's reproached for something I've heard several times, for not confining himself to American or British language, but using both. But partly it's his translators, so that his British translator, Myers, has "wanker," I think, in one poem. Americans frown at this lapse. "Wanker" is a great British word that I think Joseph might have gone for anyway, even without Myers, just from being an opportunist. And I think you have to be that. Again, it's sort of an attack on the genuine. You know he's not going to have a primary and exclusive relationship with the language, he's not going to give you purity of diction in English verse. That's not the point of him. I remember thinking how glad I was that Brodsky had fetched up in America, because here the language is bigger and jazzier and more colorful. I think British would have been too small for him; he would have been cramped in there. He said, "freedom is a library." And you just exploit it or ransack it in that spirit. I think it's wonderful.

Holland: You know that argument that Shakespeare's

English is so remarkable he must have been a Dutchman?

Hofmann: Oh, I love that.

Holland: Obviously he was a Dutchman and learned English later.

Hofmann: Yes, of course! It stands to reason....I just reviewed a book by a British poet called Charles Boyle, who I think sees that this is an interesting way of coming at things. I remember he describes a "lingering pink over Acton that seems reluctant to call it a day." And I wrote about that. I praised it for its almost alien or foreign consciousness of idiom. It sounds like something you were taught at language school that afternoon, and you practice it in a poem! I think Simic—whom Charles Boyle and I and others admire a lot—writes like that sometimes. You think of a playwright and you think of Stoppard, who was born in Czechoslovakia. The other, the example of the native, would be Pinter. With him it's become a study, a specialism, making, reusing, hollowing out these phrases that people quite unreflectively use in English. He's sort of made that a study, as I've said. Whereas Stoppard is more flamboyant, more outrageous.

Thomas: I'm curious to know what you were reading growing up in England. American poets, British poets?

Hofmann: Not British. I mean, deliberately not British, because I thought no amount of British poetry would make me into a British poet. Also, I now see that I got a lot of that at school: Larkin and Auden and so on. No, I read Americans and I read Germans deliberately to supplement myself. I also have a thing with American because

I lived here for a couple of years as a kid. In essence, I merged American and German. So the people I read when I started were Pound, when I was seventeen, the short stuff. It was, I suppose, the primary pleasure in words. It's like the idiom thing: you have just four plain lines, and in the middle of it there's something gaudy or very often something Latinate that just sets the whole thing in flame. "The Temperaments," "The Tea Shop," "Les Millwin," the "Salutations," wonderful things. So much nowadays has to do with not the common way of saying something, but the slightly uncomfortable or original or zany way of saying something. And I think a lot of that goes back to Pound....As a student I read Lowell and Enzensberger. Basically, I wanted to write a cross of the two. The perception of Enzensberger and the splendor of Lowell.

Thomas: Do you see the studies in the first part of *Corona, Corona*, the poems about Crassus and Richard Dadd, Beckmann, Crane, Schwitters, Gaye, as Lowellian?

Hofmann: *Life Studies*, part three. Honestly, I'd never thought of that. How odd of me. But then I'm this mixture of self-consciousness and a sort of cluelessness. In a way you have to be. Doesn't Lowell say something about the poet being "over-armored and on to what he does"?....I suppose so. I suppose there's the portrait in which the portraitist sees himself, and that's the point of them. But I hadn't seen them as just versions of my meager self.

Thomas: One thing I noticed about those poems is that they end abruptly. I found myself looking for another stanza or two, turning the page even, only to discover that the last stanza I'd read was the last stanza.

Hofmann: You'd had your lot.

Thomas: Are you aware of that as a strategy?

Hofmann: Not really, no. No. I remember Alan Hollinghurst, one of the first times I was reviewed, he wrote on that *Poetry Introduction* volume that came out in '82, "These poems also end in the most surprising way." And that was the end of the review. I was looking for a couple more paragraphs as well. I thought, come on, a little detail here, a little exposition....Hm, not really, no, because it seems to me enough. My judgment is that that's enough then. It may be my aesthetic or something, but it's not a strategy, a gambit. My father used to tell me this story about Henry James dining out for a year, people telling him stories. And occasionally he'd say, "Stop, I don't want to hear any more. Don't tell me the ending." And he would go away and let his imagination work on what he'd been given.

I show students this letter that Elizabeth Bishop wrote to an unknown student—it's right at the end of the *Letters*—and the girl is interested in writing, and she wants to know what to do, what to read, and Bishop tells her to read old things, and to read a poet's complete works, and their letters, and when you write, she says, remember that the mistake people make is they go on too long. I think poems of mine on occasion have gone on too long. They didn't pan out, so I cut them. I truncate. You could say it's like Rilke, the "Archaic Torso," you know: you may just have a torso. You must change your ending.

Thomas: When James, though, stopped a story, it was presumably to imagine the end of the narrative. Do you think your way of stopping poems at surprising moments has to do with the absence of narrative?

Hofmann: I think it very much has to do with narrative being compromised or narrative not being espoused all along the line. So it's sort of amalgam of image and narration. I love Lowell's lines: "We were kind of religious. We thought in images." You don't want to get to the point where the images are just sort of being trailed along by their hair....I like asking the reader to do things. I think it's very odd how little happens when you read, when people read. Particularly when people read description. You know, the author says to himself, "Oh hell, I'll throw in a paragraph of description," and you don't bear any sense of it. Somehow when doing translation of things or of circumstances into words something needs to happen. The words have to be enhanced or made more autonomous. And I think that something I've discovered over the last seven years or so is that straightforward transcription of things doesn't work. It's boring, and to the reader it doesn't happen. I think about diction and surprise and tempo. I love those poor despised things adjectives.

An adjective is a gratuitous word—that can mean it's completely null if it's a bad one, but a good (in context) adjective is a galvanising thing. It presents an idea in one word. And I think even though the reader is left on his own more by me, and has in a way more freedom, more liberty, more discretion, it might end up with me being read more as I'd like to be or as I need to be than if I guided him, guided the reader, by the hand.

Thomas: Would you see this part of a line from "On the Beach at Thorpeness" as an example: "triune reliable fissile block"?

Hofmann: Yeah.

Thomas: Each of the words having a kind of autonomy?

Hofmann: Yeah. Well, this is something from Christopher Ricks, whom I learned an awful lot from, in spite of ourselves. I read Lowell with him. And one of the things he told me which I think is true, is when you use a word all sorts of things go through a reader's mind, up to and including the opposite! So when I say that line, the reader will see "unreliable" and especially those letters "un."

Thomas: Do you think that kind of linguistic play in the mind of the reader occurs automatically, or does it have to be established by the context? For instance, when you say in the previous lines of that poem, "I looked idly right for corpses in the underbrush,/then left, to check that Sizewell was still there," that idea, put against the word reliable, almost invokes the negative prefix.

Hofmann: Yes, I don't think it happens automatically. The writer has to be putting things down in either quite a speculative or quite an undercutting sort of way. That's the thing about writing—these tiny subliminal tugs. Sometimes it can be done by a vacuum. I think of another of Lowell's songs, which begins, "Pale ale, molar, drain." "Pale ale, molar, drain." That works more by the sound of it, but there is a sort of...vacuum. The sense is a vacuum. I don't know what it's about, but it's absolutely mesmerizing, and I think that's the game.

Holland: You say something similar in "On the Beach at

Thorpeness," the lines, "My tracks were oval holes/like whole notes or snowshoes or Dover soles." That was when you read Lowell?
Hofmann: Yes: these holes, all these round things.
Holland: Particularly after "The North Sea was...yeasty, sudsy...," then you have all sorts of good sounds. But it's all "jaw jaw."
Hofmann: Yes. "Jaw jaw. War war."
Thomas: Is that Churchill?
Hofmann: That's Churchill, yeah. He says jaw jaw is better than war war. I've left out the connective. My usual operation....But I think it's interest; it's the indebtedness to be interesting. With Brodsky the rhyme thing is in the interest of memorableness. I think my own god is interest.
Holland: Henry James: "You've got to do three things. Your prose has got to be interesting, interesting, interesting."
Hofmann: Does he say that? I love that.
Thomas: I'd like to ask you briefly about your work as a reviewer. You tend to speak your mind openly about books you don't like. How do you see your role as a reviewer of books of poetry?
Hofmann: It's something I've come back to; I reviewed for a while in my early twenties. I wrote about poetry for a defunct English magazine called *Quarto*. That was just shrillness and fearlessness. But recently, in the last two or three years, I've taken it up again. And I think recently, towards poetry, I've felt I know my mind now, and I've felt impatient as well as secure. I want to confront things, I want to take issue with books that are coming out. I don't

see any reason not to. I'm interested in my response to things. I didn't want to duck out of it or leave it to other people, even when I think, Who on earth asked you to say the emperor has no clothes? I suppose I think also that if I didn't do it, actually nobody would. I feel like I have enough experience, and I sort of have this security now. Before, I didn't necessarily. It wasn't that I was necessarily timid or evasive, but I didn't welcome confrontation. But now it doesn't bother me.

Books by Michael Hofmann

Poetry

Nights in the Iron Hotel, Faber and Faber, 1983.
Acrimony, Faber and Faber, 1986.
K.S. in Lakeland: New and Selected Poems, Ecco, 1990.
Corona, Corona, Faber and Faber, 1993.
Approximately Nowhere, Faber and Faber, 1999.

Prose

Behind the Lines: Pieces on Writing and Pictures, Faber and Faber, 2001.

Translations

Beat Sterchi, *Blosch,* Faber and Faber, 1988.
Bertold Brecht, *The Good Person of Sichuan*, Methuen, 1989.
Joseph Roth, *Right and Left*, Chatto and Windus, 1991.
Hugo von Hofmannsthal, *The Lord Chandos Letter*, Penguin, 1995.
Gert Hofmann, *The Film Explainer*, Secker and Warburg, 1995.
Franz Kafka, *The Man Who Disappeared [Amerika]*, Penguin, 1996.
Joseph Roth, *The String of Pearls*, Granta Books, 1996.
Herta Muller, *The Land of Green Plums*, Metropolitan Books, 1996.
Joseph Roth, *The Tale of the 1002nd Night*, St. Martin's Press, 1998.
Zoe Jenny, *The Pollen Room*, Bloomsbury, 1998.
Joseph Roth, *Rebellion*, St. Martin's Press, 1999.
Joseph Roth, *The Legend of the Holy Drinker*, Granta Books, 2000.
Wim Wenders, *My Time with Antonioni*, Faber and Faber, 2000.
Wolfgang Koeppen, *The Hothouse*, Norton, 2001.
Joseph Roth, *The Wandering Jews*, Norton, 2001.

Anthologies

After Ovid: New Metamorphoses, edited with James Lasdun, Farrar, Straus and Giroux, 1994.

Editions

Robert Lowell (Poet to Poet), selected, Faber and Faber, 2001.

David Ferry was born in 1924 in Orange, New Jersey, educated in Maplewood, New Jersey, and at Amherst College and Harvard. From 1943 to 1946 he served as a sergeant in the United States Army Air Force. In 1958 he married Anne Ferry, a well known critic of English poetry. He taught at Wellesley College from 1952 to 1989, where he was for years the chairman of the English department. His title there is now Sophie Chantal Hart Professor of English, Emeritus. He has won several awards for his work, including the Ingram Merrill Award for Poetry and Translation, the Lenore Marshall Poetry Prize, given by the Academy of American Poets, and the Rebekah Johnson Bobbitt National Prize for Poetry, given by the Library of Congress. In 2001 he received an Award in Literature from the American Academy of Arts and Letters.

David Ferry

Brandon Cody: At what age did you decide to become a writer? What events led you to want to be a writer?
Ferry: I got started in graduate school. I guess it was having to write a Ph.D thesis, and enjoying the experience, that made me have ambitions to be a writer. I thought I was going to end up as a scholar, and I did become an author that way—I wrote a book about Wordsworth, which was a revision of my thesis. But I got interested in writing poems because I was reading a lot of poems. I think I do recall scraps of things, furtive scribblings of a few lines when I was in high school and college, but nothing that was evidence that put writing poems at the center of my interest. But I had begun to get more and more literary in college, at Amherst, because I had a couple of really great teachers there, Reuben Brower and César Lombardi Barber. So I was developing in that direction. But, as I've said, I didn't really start to write poems until I was in graduate school. The first poem I really worked on and finished was "The Embarkation for Cythera." It got

published in the *Kenyon Review*, then edited by the poet John Crowe Ransom, one of my idols, and that was a thrill. A very big thrill.

Justin Elswit: I think you started out doing a lot of translations. How did you move from being a translator to writing your own stuff?

Ferry: It's the other way around, really. There's one translation in my first book, a translation of a poem by Ronsard, a famous one—"Quand vous serez bien vieille," and then in my second book—and there's a long gap between my first book and my second because—I don't know why—I wasn't writing very much and I was doing a lot of other things as a teacher at Wellesley College—there were three translations, one of them an ode of Horace, the only one I knew at that point. I don't even remember how I got into doing that one, but I did it. There was also the translation of a poem by Jorge Guillén, a distinguished Spanish poet, who was teaching at Wellesley, in exile from Franco's Spain. And there was a short poem by Eugenio Montale. Then in the next book, *Dwelling Places: Poems and Translations*, the mix was about half and half, so in other words I was moving in the direction of being a translator as well as a poet. In my new book, *Of No Country I Know: New and Selected Poems and Translations*, in the new part of it the mix is once again about half and half. I've made an effort, both in this new book and in *Dwelling Places* to make connections between the poems and the translations. Friends began to help me by suggestions of poems to translate that they thought would go with the poems I was working on and that would go with the general character of the book I was working on. In most cases I tried to be as faithful as possible in my translations, but some were more free, shaped and somewhat changed to fit the purposes of the book as I was conceiving of it.

During this last decade I've also produced some books that are purely translation: my rendering of the Gilgamesh epic, my translations of the Odes of Horace and the Eclogues of Virgil, and, just finished, the Epistles of Horace. I got interested in the Gilgamesh material through a friend, the Assyriologist William Moran, and in the Horace material through another friend, the classicist Donald Carne-Ross. In both cases I started out with a few passages or poems suggested by them and then I got hooked and did the whole kit and kaboodle.

Allison Ellsworth: What about other people's writing draws you to do translation and to do responses? There are a number of poems in this collection that are responses—like Johnson on Pope and a number of others—and poems from your father's writings and your grandfather's.

Ferry: I think I'd say two or three things about that. I tend to be a hero-worshipper of some writers, and Dr. Johnson is one of them. So I was very interested in everything of his that I could find and when I had begun translating a little Latin I became aware of two or three translations that Johnson did of Horace, early in his career. He wrote the poem I called "The Lesson" in his old age. It's about parental love, telling how his father took him out and tried to teach him to swim, and how he wasn't good at it.

It fit with some other poems in the book, like my poem "A Young Woman" and "Goodnight." So I responded to the Johnson poem out of admiration of him but also because it suited my bookmaking purposes.

As for using other people's writing—I guess you're referring to "After Spotsylvania Court House" and "Counterpart," two poems which derive from and quote from letters I found in my father's apartment after he died. Finding them was a useful accident. All I know of my great-grandfather and of any kind of connection with American history that I've got is through writing, through letters and through photographs (which are a kind of writing). My great-grandfather was a Methodist preacher who went down to Virginia after the bloody battle of Spotsylvania Court House, in 1864, and wrote letters home to his wife using a kind of nineteenth century idealist language—"It is a wonderful honor to be here and to do good"—that kind of wholehearted language I found both admirable and endearing, and also naive in a way that didn't destroy my admiration of it. It was my link to a past that meant something to me, and the poem "Graveyard," about a photograph of my father was another sort of link. I also found that photograph in his apartment after his death. Links to the past, through writing. It's what you have left.

Michael Kennedy: I'm wondering why don't you write about your close family—your wife, your daughter, and your son—as you did about your great-grandfather?

Ferry: There's a poem in *Strangers*, "On a Sunday Morning," that's about my son. There's a poem in *Dwelling Places*, "A Young Woman," that's decidedly about my daughter. In fact, I wrote it because my daughter said to me, How come you never wrote a poem about me? And so I wrote the poem about her, and showed it to her, and it was only several days later that she came to that it was about her. The dedicatory poem in this new book, not a poem by me but a medieval poem adapted by me, is about our marriage. So's the poem "Aubade" in my first book and the poem "A Tomb at Tarquinia," in *Strangers*. But you're quite right that, compared to some other ways that I've written, there are relatively few such poems. I'm not sure of the answer to that, except that I think there are some ways in which it's easier to write when the writing is deflected into some other circumstance than the most immediately personal ones. It's easier to write about the dead or to write about a great-grandfather because it's harder to formulate what's here and immediate, right up close. I do have intentions of writing more often in more personal ways. But this is only one of my intentions.

As you know from reading my book, there's a lot of interest in photography in some of these poems. My son is a wonderful photojournalist and there have been times when I wanted to get into writing some direct responses to the work he's been doing, often in harrowing situations. But there's a kind of shyness on my part that enters into it: not wanting to scribble across the surface of his remarkable work.

Elizabeth Howie: I was wondering why you go back to the

Bible. For example, in the poem "The Proselyte" you use the phrase "unclean spirits." I was wondering, did you derive inspiration from the Bible? Is that the reason you go back to it?

Ferry: Certainly for the purpose of the poem you're referring to, that one passage from the New Testament has been very important for me, the anecdote about the wild man, crazy man, the very marginal character who was on the edge of the town and Jesus came upon him and the unclean spirits in him were crying, "Torment me not!" and Jesus called them out of his body and into the bodies of the Gadarene swine, who then rushed into the waters and were drowned. It's a very compelling story. When I was writing *Dwelling Places* and doing a lot of writing about street people I was also doing —I think I talked about this the last time I was here—a certain amount of reading about wild men, all the medieval and ancient writing and art about wild men— Nebuchadnezzar the king out eating grass, Enkidu the wild man in the Gilgamesh story I rendered. The connection between this kind of reading and the New Testament story came about that way. I don't think of myself as in general as strikingly more of a Biblical reader than most people, so it's more a matter of a particular raid into some useful material. On the other hand I guess I *am* influenced in a way by the strong Methodist-preacher-missionary strain in my father's family. I suppose the Bible gets into my head by that route, though not very systematically. Also, the context for some of my poems about street people is the supper program we help run at a church in Boston, so it's no surprise that a biblical vocabulary gets into those poems. It's been more a question of what I've found compelling and useful for the purposes of some particular poem.

Michael Doherty: Are there any other authors or poets who have inspired you to write or whom you want to model your writing after?

Ferry: I think my double answer to that would be that I can right away think of the American poets and the English poets of the now-past twentieth century whom I find myself admiring most, and that's a very clear, obvious list—Robert Frost, Wallace Stevens—when I was an undergraduate I wrote my honor's thesis on Stevens, he and Frost were the first modern poets whose work really took hold of me—Thomas Hardy, Philip Larkin, Elizabeth Bishop, William Carlos Williams. The other side of the story, of course, is the worry of ending up sounding like an imitation of somebody you admire. It's almost like saying that my list of people I admire is my list of people I don't want to sound like. And I'm sure I end up, in an inferior way, sounding like some of them at various times.

Then I'd have to double back again and say there's another kind of answer to your question. Much as you want to find your own voice and differentiate yourself even from, and maybe especially from, the people you admire the most, poetry (and any other kind of writing) is made out of what's in your ear, your memories of what language sounds like in various situations. If you're writing in any form you've got in your ear the cadences you've heard in other people's use of that form, and so while trying to avoid sounding like somebody else you're at the same time using the way the English language has behaved rhythmically as you've heard it elsewhere. We don't make up anything in our language. It's all, in a sense, memory. It's, as Frost says, "things that live in the cave of the mouth," that were always there. You don't make it out of nothing. You make language out of language. It's both trying not to sound like other people and using ad hoc what's gotten into your ear.

Kristin Tyman: How much time do you devote to writing or research in a week, and when you're writing, is there a certain place where you feel most comfortable?

Ferry: Yeah, in front the computer in my study. I work on writing some of most mornings, and one of the great things about doing more and more translating is that it gives you something to do on those days—and those are most days—when you don't have any ideas about what you're doing with your own writing. Translating gives you something to do that's very useful because it puts into your ear useful pieces of language, useful cadences, useful habits of writing. So I work part of every morning in a kind of scrappy way. I have a piano right downstairs under where I work, so I go down and play the piano a lot and then I go back up and sit in front of the screen and try something else out. Sometimes I work like this all afternoon too, but often I don't because I have other stuff to do, chores, letters, prose obligations.

Ali Gorski: I was wondering how you feel about revising

poems—whether once you've published them you leave them in that form, or whether you think of revising them over the years.

Ferry: When I put together this new and selected volume, I looked very hard at my first book, and I revised it drastically. I left out a lot of it, and rewrote some of it. I kept all the poems in the two later books (*Strangers* and *Dwelling Places*) almost without change. There's one poem, "Caprimulgidae," that I'd been very unhappy with, it wasn't working, and I redid that one and now I feel better about it. There are a number of poems in my books that were changed between the time of their magazine publication and their inclusion in the books. After that I usually left them alone. But of course there are almost no poems where I couldn't think over and over again about some possible revision or another. There comes a time, though, when you say, let it be. But it's hard for me to distinguish between the process of writing and the process of revising. One you get something down on paper, everything else feels like a revision of it.

Chris Bilello: Is there any poetry that you write just for yourself, for your own benefit, that you don't publish?

Ferry: I have a number of things in notebooks that I'm hoping someday to finish. I'm such a slow writer and such a reviser that almost everything that I've gotten to the point where you could call it a poem has ended up in the book. I don't have a big supply of alternatives. I kind of wish I did, but I don't. Some of my poems I've worked on for twenty years, thirty years, I don't care. They're sort of sitting around and finally I get it done. But my notebook of other stuff is small.

Elswit: How would you describe the changes in both your writing style and the subject of your poems from when you started writing in graduate school to some of the new poems?

Ferry: The most important change for me took place right in the middle of that first book. It's a little hard to describe the change now because for the purposes of the new book, *Of No Country I Know*, I changed the order of poems from *On the Way to the Island*, that first book. There they occurred more or less in what I could remember as the chronological order I wrote them in. The poems in the first half are a good deal more elaborate in texture than the poems later on, and they tend to be about situations that occur inside other works of art. "The Embarkation for Cythera," for example, the first poem I ever wrote, is based on a painting by Watteau, and another poem, "On the Way to the Island," is related to that one. They're very much more "art" than most of the plainer poems later in the second half of that book. So, generally speaking, I took that turn rather early in my career. I think the poems in the second half of that book, as it was originally printed, are more like poems I've been doing ever since.

Anna Bacon: I think it's interesting that you've written in many different forms. You've done a sestina and sonnets and the *Gilgamesh* in couplets. I know that the sestina is difficult because you have to use the same words, and I was wondering if that poem was a struggle for you. Did you find that you had to force it to incorporate the six words? Also, do you have a favorite form? And, finally, how do you choose the form that a poem is going to be in?

Ferry: The sestina is certainly not my favorite form. I hope never to write another one. I think that the last time I was here I quoted Richard Wilbur as saying that the sestina form is a horrid doily. In the case of "The Guest Ellen at the Supper for Street People," though, the poem keeps asking questions over and over, obsessively, and the lives of the people being looked at are the same over and over—"the quotidian," the dailyness, "of unending torment." I began to find that in the lines I was writing into the computer the same vocabulary tended to occur—words like "torment," "enchantment," "body," "voice," and so one, and a lot of them began to occur at the ends of lines (which always tend to be emphasized in one way or another), and all of a sudden—I have a note on the computer where I said to myself, what if this turned into a sestina?—and so I looked up the sestina form, because like everybody else I had trouble remembering what it was, and I began to reshape the poem in that direction, because in this instance the sestina form, obsessive and insistent and repetitive, seemed particularly appropriate. Often the form just seems like an academic exercise. There are very great sestinas, though. Elizabeth Bishop's poem called "Sestina" is one. Sir Philip Sidney's double sestina, "Ye Goatherd Gods," is another.

If I thought about what a favorite form for me is, I suppose the form I have found myself writing in most often, or more often than others, is unrhymed iambic pentameter, and often unrhymed iambic pentameter arranged in couplets. Because I learned from the Gilgamesh experience. I started trying to do that one in blank verse, that is to say, in uninterrupted paragraphs of unrhymed pentameter lines, and it was very heavy. I couldn't get it to go. But when I started putting it into couplets it sort of oxygenated the verse, aerated it. I could see what I was doing. I could get at it. The poem began to move. And so I've used the form quite a lot. A part of that is that one of the poets I most admire in the world is the 18th century poet Alexander Pope, and I most admire him for the focus and intensity of the workmanship within a recognizably framed form, the so-called heroic couplet, the rhymed iambic pentameter couplet. Rhyming at that length is something I would shy away from doing systematically, but the idea of the couplet, the idea of a form that's plain, most like talk, and at the same time a highly, complexly, usable art form, was something I could really work with, and so I've used it pretty often.

Jason Pokrant: You seem to enjoy very much what you do. But looking back now, is there anything you regret or would change, whether it be in your style, form, or your profession entirely, or would you do everything the same if you could do it again?

Ferry: I would write a lot more. I don't know what I was doing about writing in the years between my first book and my second, and I very much regret that I didn't build up more of a stock of material in that period. I can't explain how that happened, or rather didn't happen, but it's something I regret. Naturally, I think probably I have the feeling that everybody has over work they've done, that there's a mixture of pleasure that you did something, inevitably combined with a feeling that, well, it could have been better. I don't know how I would particularize it further, but I bet you recognize that feeling about work. But it's mostly a quantitative matter. I wish I had done more poems of my own and there are a lot of other translations I would like to do—that I'll still do. But it would be nice to have even more of it done.

Kennedy: Your poems seem to describe a picture so well, you seem always to be able to get a perfect picture into the reader's mind. How do you get a poem started? Do you sit at your computer and remember something that's happened in the past, or do you see something happen and try to turn it into a poem?

Ferry: Thank you. It varies a lot. Sometimes I have a line hanging around in my head, and just sort of getting that line onto the computer and fooling around with it gets something going. Very often it doesn't get something going, at least not that year. But it's still there in the computer. In the old days, before the computer, it was still there in a notebook. Sometimes I've written out something that I wanted to get said, in prose, and then worked from that prose to see what a viable way of getting it into lines that had some music in them was going to be. With *Dwelling Places*—well, really with the last three books, starting with *Strangers*—after a certain point in the writing of a book I began to see that it was going to turn into a book, with a certain character of its own, or a certain kind of prevailing subject matter. In the case of *Dwelling Places*, people who didn't have dwelling places and people who did. And that led to some governing ideas for poems, and led me to look, as I said earlier, for relevant things to translate. I can't say I always start from the same kind of point, because I don't.

Ellsworth: When you last spoke with us you mentioned having been in the army. How did that affect your writing, if it did at all?

Ferry: Hardly at all, I think, except in the poem called "The Soldier." The army experience I had was extremely lucky. This was World War II. I was mainly stationed in England, well out of harm's way. So, because of my luck, I didn't have the sort of war material that some other poets of that generation had. The effect of the army was minimal, at least as it relates to my poetry. Except that—I don't know exactly how this bore on the poetry or not—but because I was in the army between my freshman and sophomore years in college I came back, like a lot of people at that time, as a lot older sophomore than I would have been otherwise, and a somewhat different person. And that made me, I think, a more serious reader, and reading led to all the rest.

Tyman: When you have a dry spell with your writing, do you ever get anxious or nervous?

Ferry: Very.

Tyman: How do you cope?

Ferry: I don't. I just kvetch a lot. But, as I said earlier, translation is helpful. It gives me something to do. I'm translating the Epistles of Horace now, a big work. I'm getting near the end of it and I'm getting a little anxious, because I need another big translation project. I'm fooling around with some of the Satires of Horace, to see if that's what I'm going to want to do, and I'm fooling around with the first Georgic of Virgil. I don't know which I'm going to get into, the Horace or the Virgil, but I need one or the other, both because I love being a translator and also because translating helps with dry periods.

In fact, I can't really make a distinction that's all that clear between being a poet and being a translator. There's the big difference, of course, that Horace or Virgil had the original idea and that they're a lot better than me, so I admire them and fall in love with them. But once you've got the translation going it's like having a rough draft of a poem that you're working on, and your experience of the activity is remarkably the same. So translating gives you the illusion—and it's not entirely an illusion—that there isn't a dry period after all.

Gorski: Some of the poems that we've read take place in and around Cambridge. Has Cambridge had an impact on your poetry?

Ferry: It sure has, in those poems. I thought during one dry period that I might make a whole book of poems about Ellery Street, the street I live on. But I shied away from that, partly because I knew I probably couldn't do it. I just don't work that systematically and also I kind of hate ideas for a book, topics, that are that tightly defined. But

I did think about it, and there are several other poems, beside the one called “Ellery Street,” that are about my immediate neighborhood.

Cambridge is extremely important to me because it has people I talk about poetry with a lot, and other translators and writers; it’s got people like Harry in it, and Christopher Ricks, people I love to talk about these things with. There are other poets. It’s a very good community for poets. There are lots of generous-minded people around. We do a lot of exchanging of things. So Cambridge is extremely important for me, and Boston as well.

Ellsworth: When you are translating, do you tend to try to emulate the style of the original writer of the poem, or do you tend to try to make the poem your own?

Ferry: I have a couple of ways of talking about that. Certainly I try to be as faithful as possible to the poem. Let me come back to that point in a second, after I confess that there are some poems where I’ve taken certain liberties in order to suit my purposes in making a book. Rilke’s “Song of a Drunkard” is an example. He has his drunkard say:

> Es war nicht in mir. Es ging aus und ein.
> Da wollt ich es halten. Da hielt es der Wein.
> (Ich weiss nicht mehr, was es war.)
> Dann hielt er mir jenes und hielt mir dies
> bis ich mich ganz auf ihn verliess.
> Ich Narr.

I translated the stanza as:

I don't know what it was I wanted to hold onto.
I kept losing it and I didn't know what it was
Except I wanted to hold onto it. The drink kept it in,
So at least for awhile I felt as if I had it,
Whatever it was. But it was the drink that had it
And held it and had hold of me too. Asshole.

"Ich Narr" is "I fool" or "I was a fool" or "I'm a fool," any one of which sounded awkward to me in my poem, and untrue to the voice I wanted for the poem as placed among other poems about street people in that section of my book. "Asshole" seemed to me what the voice would say. But it also seems to me to be true to the tone of Rilke's poem. At least I persuade myself that that's so. But I do acknowledge that from somebody's point of view—maybe Rilke's —I've taken a liberty in this case.

I do sincerely mean that as a translator I want to be as true as possible, as faithful as possible, to the poem I'm translating. But there are built-in limitations. One is the limitation of talent. I only translate great poems and of course I know I'm not good enough. (It's some comfort that I think nobody else is, either.) Then there are the differences of language. In translating Horace or Virgil I make no attempt to imitate the Latin meters systematically, because the whole system of Latin meter is so different from English meter, but I do try very hard to find some kind of equivalent for the tones of voice that I hear in the original; I try to respect and use and responsibly interpret the detailed narrative, the situations, the figures of speech I find there, and to use English meters that have some aspects of equivalence. This is true for most of the other translations I've done, from other languages. A translation can't carry the original bodily over the line. It's a form of reading, of interpretation, but my hope is that it's faithful reading, faithful interpretation.

Books by David Ferry

Poetry

On the Way to the Island, Wesleyan University Press, 1960.

Strangers: A Book of Poems, University of Chicago Press, 1983.

Dwelling Places: Poems and Translations, University of Chicago Press, 1993.

Of No Country I Know: New and Selected Poems and Translations, University of Chicago Press, 1999.

Prose

The Limits of Mortality: An Essay on Wordsworth's Major Poems, Wesleyan University Press, 1959.

Translations

Gilgamesh: A New Rendering in English Verse, Farrar, Straus and Giroux, 1992.

The Odes of Horace, Farrar, Straus and Giroux, 1997.

The Eclogues of Virgil, Farrar, Straus and Giroux, 1999.

The Epistles of Horace, Farrar Straus and Giroux, 2001.

Editions

Wordsworth, selected, Dell, 1959.

British Literature, co-editor, D.C. Heath, 1974.